The Visual Dictionary of Pre-Press & Production

An AVA Book

Published by AVA Publishing SA
Rue des Fontenailles 16
Case Postale
1000 Lausanne 6
Switzerland
Tel: +41 786 005 109
Email: enquiries@avabooks.ch

Distributed by Thames & Hudson (ex-North America)
181a High Holborn
London WC1V 7QX
United Kingdom
Tel: +44 20 7845 5000 Fax: +44 20 7845 5055
Email: sales@thameshudson.co.uk
www.thamesandhudson.com

Distributed in the USA & Canada by:
Ingram Publisher Services Inc.
1 Ingram Blvd.
La Vergne TN 37086
USA
Tel: +1 866 400 5351 Fax: +1 800 838 1149
Email: customer.service@ingrampublisherservices.com

English Language Support Office
AVA Publishing (UK) Ltd.
Tel: +44 1903 204 455
Email: enquiries@avabooks.ch

ISBN 978-2-940411-29-0

10 9 8 7 6 5 4 3 2 1

Design by Gavin Ambrose www.gavinambrose.co.uk

Production by AVA Book Production Pte. Ltd., Singapore
Tel: +65 6334 8173 Fax: +65 6259 9830
Email: production@avabooks.com.sg

Gavin Ambrose & Paul Harris

The Visual Dictionary of Pre-Press & Production

How to get the most out of this book

This book is an easy-to-use reference to the key terms used in the pre-press production processes for print and digital work. Each entry comprises a brief textual definition along with an illustration or visual example. Supplementary contextual information is also provided.

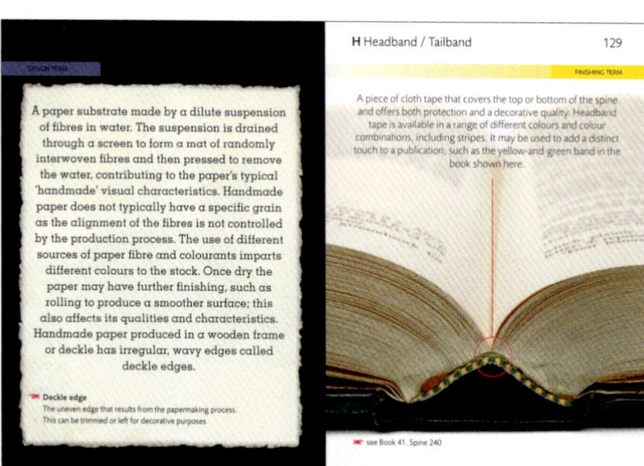

DESIGN TERM

A paper substrate made by a dilute suspension of fibres in water. The suspension is drained through a screen to form a mat of randomly interwoven fibres and then pressed to remove the water, contributing to the paper's typical 'handmade' visual characteristics. Handmade paper does not typically have a specific grain as the alignment of the fibres is not controlled by the production process. The use of different sources of paper fibre and colourants imparts different colours to the stock. Once dry the paper may have further finishing, such as rolling to produce a smoother surface; this also affects its qualities and characteristics. Handmade paper produced in a wooden frame or deckle has irregular, wavy edges called deckle edges.

Deckle edge
The uneven edge that results from the papermaking process. This can be trimmed or left for decorative purposes

H Headband / Tailband 129

FINISHING TERM

A piece of cloth tape that covers the top or bottom of the spine and offers both protection and a decorative quality. Headband tape is available in a range of different colours and colour combinations, including stripes. It may be used to add a distinct touch to a publication, such as the yellow-and-green band in the book shown here.

see Book 41, Spine 240

Key areas addressed in this book are those terms commonly used in reference to the study of pre-press production processes.

Entries are presented in alphabetical order and identified in one of four categories – design, screen, printing and finishing – to provide an easy reference system.

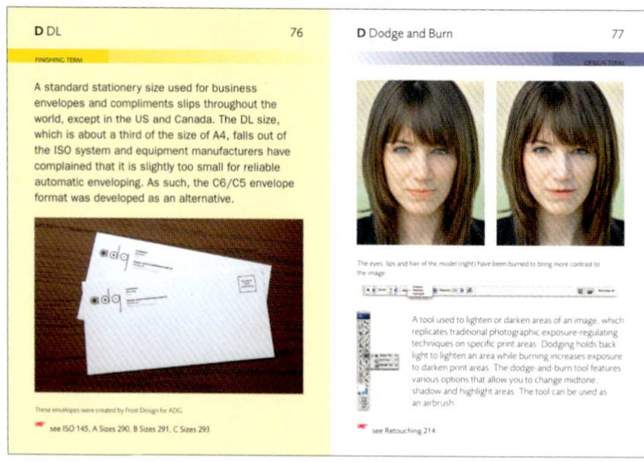

D DL 76

FINISHING TERM

A standard stationery size used for business envelopes and compliments slips throughout the world, except in the US and Canada. The DL size, which is about a third of the size of A4, falls out of the ISO system and equipment manufacturers have complained that it is slightly too small for reliable automatic enveloping. As such, the C6/C5 envelope format was developed as an alternative.

These envelopes were created by Frost Design for ADG

see ISO 145, A Sizes 290, B Sizes 291, C Sizes 293

D Dodge and Burn 77

DESIGN TERM

The eyes, lips and hair of the model (right) have been burned to bring more contrast to the image

A tool used to lighten or darken areas of an image, which replicates traditional photographic exposure-regulating techniques on specific print areas. Dodging holds back light to lighten an area while burning increases exposure to darken print areas. The dodge-and-burn tool features various options that allow you to change midtone, shadow and highlight areas. The tool can be used as an airbrush.

see Retouching 214

O Overprinting 182

PRINTING TERM

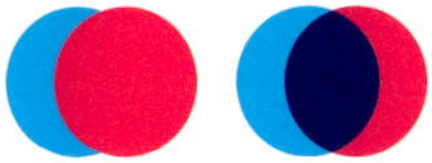

Without overprinting

With overprinting

The printing of one ink over another to create different colours. Overprinting can be used for creative effects and to extend colour options when printing with a limited range, such as two colours. The illustration above shows two colours without overprinting (left) and with overprinting (right). Notice how the two colours create a third colour when they overprint. In this instance, the new colour is blue. According to colour theory, overprinting pairs of the three subtractive primary CMY process colours produces additive primary colours. To overprint effectively, a designer needs to bear in mind the order in which the process colours print. If printing in the order cyan, magenta, yellow and black, the yellow cannot overprint cyan, for example. Blacks with different tones and intensities can also be achieved with overprinting.

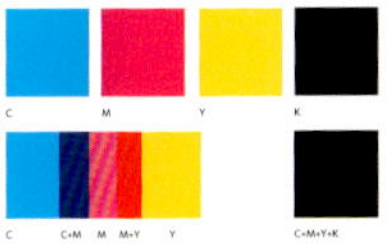

C M Y K

C C+M M M+Y Y C+M+Y+K

The top row of swatch chips shows each of the subtractive CMYK primary colours. The bottom row shows magenta overprinting cyan to create blue, and yellow overprinting magenta to create red. The final swatch chip shows a four-colour black. Notice how it has a deeper, more intense colour than the single colour black above it.

P Padding 183

SCREEN TERM

The empty space that surrounds the content on a printed page or webpage. On a printed page, padding is the space between columns and images. A page can be specified in one of two ways: the image columns can be fixed and padding is the available space; or the padding is fixed and the column widths altered to use the space. In digital media, padding is equivalent to the margins of a printed page, as illustrated below. The padding separates the content from the edge of the screen and helps make it easier to read.

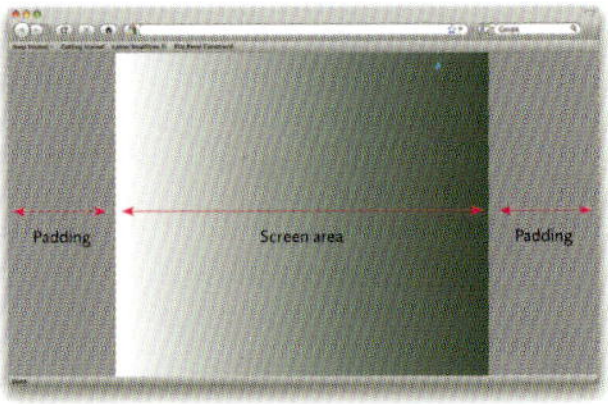

Padding Screen area Padding

Each page contains a single entry and, where appropriate, a printer's hand symbol ☛ provides page references to other related and relevant entries.

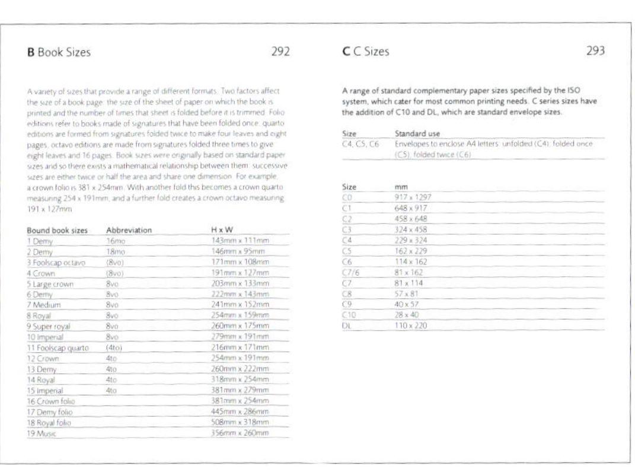

B Book Sizes 292

A variety of sizes that provide a range of different formats. Two factors affect the size of a book page: the size of the sheet of paper on which the book is printed and the number of times that sheet is folded before it is trimmed. Folio editions refer to books made of signatures that have been folded once, quarto editions are formed from signatures folded twice to make four leaves and eight pages, octavo editions are made from signatures folded three times to give eight leaves and 16 pages. Book sizes were originally based on standard paper sizes and so there exists a mathematical relationship between them: successive sizes are either twice or half the area and share one dimension. For example, a crown folio is 381 x 254mm. With another fold this becomes a crown quarto measuring 254 x 191mm, and a further fold creates a crown octavo measuring 191 x 127mm.

Bound book sizes	Abbreviation	H x W
1 Demy	16mo	143mm x 111mm
2 Demy	18mo	146mm x 95mm
3 Foolscap octavo	(8vo)	171mm x 108mm
4 Crown	(8vo)	191mm x 127mm
5 Large crown	8vo	203mm x 133mm
6 Demy	8vo	222mm x 143mm
7 Medium	8vo	241mm x 152mm
8 Royal	8vo	254mm x 159mm
9 Super royal	8vo	260mm x 175mm
10 Imperial	8vo	279mm x 191mm
11 Foolscap quarto	(4to)	216mm x 171mm
12 Crown	4to	254mm x 191mm
13 Demy	4to	260mm x 222mm
14 Royal	4to	318mm x 254mm
15 Imperial	4to	381mm x 279mm
16 Crown folio		381mm x 254mm
17 Demy folio		445mm x 286mm
18 Royal folio		508mm x 318mm
19 Music		356mm x 260mm

C C Sizes 293

A range of standard complementary paper sizes specified by the ISO system, which cater for most common printing needs. C series sizes have the addition of C10 and DL, which are standard envelope sizes.

Size	Standard use
C4, C5, C6	Envelopes to enclose A4 letters: unfolded (C4); folded once (C5); folded twice (C6)

Size	mm
C0	917 x 1297
C1	648 x 917
C2	458 x 648
C3	324 x 458
C4	229 x 324
C5	162 x 229
C6	114 x 162
C7/6	81 x 162
C7	81 x 114
C8	57 x 81
C9	40 x 57
C10	28 x 40
DL	110 x 220

A reference section provides information on various paper and typography conventions and standards.

Welcome to *The Visual Dictionary of Pre-Press & Production*, a book that provides textual definitions and visual explanations for common terms found in the disciplines of print and digital pre-press production processes, as well as pertinent entries from related disciplines.

This book aims to provide clear definitions of some of the myriad terms used within pre-press production, including explanations of commonly misused terms such as, for example, shiners and bouncers. As you might expect, *The Visual Dictionary of Pre-Press & Production* provides visual explanations from the traditional and the classic to the contemporary and experimental, including digital and web processes.

Pictured opposite are letterpress character blocks. Letterpress is discussed on page 158.

Pictured above is an envelope created by Research Studios. It features a heat emboss, which is a finishing process explained on page 87, and a button-and-string closure, which is defined on page 47.

PHOTO
IPSUS01
PLANS
IPSUS01

Pre-press includes a range of different processes and techniques that are grouped into printing, finishing, screen and design categories to further aid understanding. Many of these processes will be required; they ensure that any given design job is produced as planned.

A clear understanding of the key terms and concepts used in pre-press enable a designer to better articulate and formalise ideas, and ensure greater accuracy in the communication of those ideas to others.

With the benefit of technological developments, pre-press techniques are flourishing and represent powerful, vibrant and constantly evolving processes that add value to print and digital design production. Developments in these processes enable designers to be more creative and to have increasing control over the production of their work.

Pictured left is a brochure created by February Design for Ipsus, which features a black foil stamp on black stock. See foil blocking on page 104.

Pictured right are screens that are used for screen printing, which is discussed on pages 200 and 223.

These dictionary entries provide thought-provoking, compact and basic definitions and instructive insights into different elements of pre-press processes: important fundamental principles, methods, materials, equipment, technical advances and techniques. A broad and contextual approach to the field is established through the use of links, cross-references and parallels between entries, which is supplemented by visual explanations that expand on key terms.

The book also includes a reference section that provides a databank relating to paper size and typographical terms and standards.

Pictured right is a fashion catalogue for Sallynoggin College in Ireland. Created by Unthink, it features a yellow Singer-sewn binding that sits beneath a wraparound cover. The sewn seam adds a tactile element to the piece and also opens up a range of colour choices for the thread. Stitching and sewing techniques are explained on page 244.

Pictured below is a logotype created by February Design, which features a simulated overprint to create a sense of movement and depth. Overprinting is defined on page 182.

Intro.
We are delighted to pres
the work of our 2007
Fashion Design graduate
The graduate collections
are the result of two years

Contents

The Dictionary

Absolute measurements

Measurements of fixed values, such as a millimetre, which is a precisely defined increment of a centimetre. Both points and picas, the basic typographic measurements, are fixed values that are expressed in finite terms.

Relative measurements

Values in typography that are defined by a series of relative measurements linked to typesize. Examples include character spacing and the em. For example, type set 70pt has a 70pt em. Type set 40pt has a 40pt em.

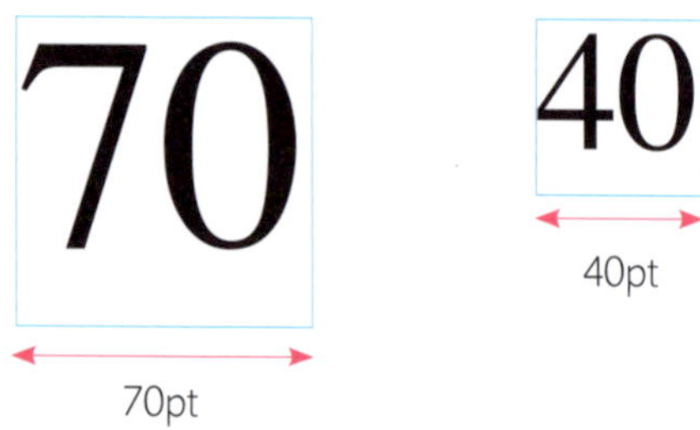

A range of symbols used in Latin languages to indicate that the sound of a letter is altered during pronunciation. Many accents are specific to certain languages; the double acute, for instance, is used solely in Hungarian and is sometimes referred to as the Hungarumlaut. Some of the main diacritic marks are shown below:

é	É	Acute	č	Č	Caron
ő	Ő	Double acute	ā	Ā	Macron
è	È	Grave	ç	Ç	Cedilla
ê	Ê	Circumflex	ą	Ą	Ogonek
ë	Ë	Umlaut / diaeresis	å	Å	Ring
ă	Ă	Breve	ȧ	Ȧ	Dot / overdot
ñ	Ñ	Tilde	ạ	Ạ	Dot / underdot

While most fonts have characters with full diacritic sets, the more graphic fonts may not. You may be asked to set an accent that doesn't exist as a drawn letterform. In these cases you will need to set the character and the floating accent next to each other and kern them together to form a single unit, as shown in the example below.

Two separate symbols can be kerned together to form a single character, in this case an underdot.

see Font / Typeface 108

SCREEN TERM

A family of computer programs, developed by Adobe Systems, which allow a user to create, view, manipulate and manage files using the Portable Document Format (PDF). Acrobat Professional can transform PostScript, Word, Powerpoint and other files to the PDF format. It has a range of settings that allow a designer to manipulate documents, such as changing image resolution to produce a smaller file size; adding comments and stipulating print settings. As many jobs are sent to print as a PDF file, the Acrobat preflight facility allows a designer to check that all the necessary elements, such as picture and font files, are present and included. Designers can specify which ISO standard to use for graphic content exchange. PDF/X standards govern print publishing workflow while PDF/A standards govern archiving and are less stringent.

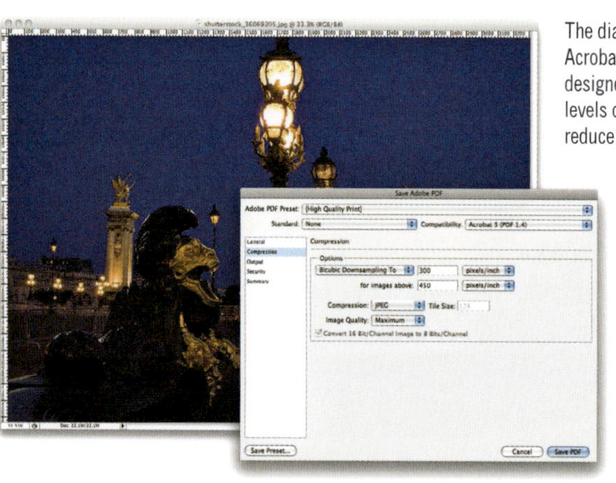

The dialog box shows how Acrobat Professional allows a designer to choose different levels of compression to reduce file size.

see Compression 60, ISO 145

DESIGN TERM

Here, the base image is left unchanged, underneath an adjustment layer that has added colour to the image. Additional adjustment layers can further alter the image while leaving the original intact.

A layer used for making changes to a digital image without affecting the original image. An adjustment layer is used to apply effects, filters or undertake image and colour correction while leaving the base image intact. Use of adjustment layers means that the base image is always available for reference, to be compared with the manipulated image. You can also revert to it, should any errors be made.

see Filters 96, Layers 155

DESIGN TERM

The position of type within a text block in relation to both vertical and horizontal margins. A designer uses alignment to work on the shape formed by the text block within the overall design.

Text can be aligned along the horizontal plane.

Range left / ragged right
This alignment follows the principle of handwriting, with text tight and aligned to the left margin and ending ragged on the right.

Centred
Each line is centrally aligned horizontally between the margins to form a symmetrical shape, with ragged beginnings and endings. Raggedness can be controlled by adjusting line endings.

Range right / ragged left
Right-aligning text is less common as it is more difficult to read, but it is used for captions and other accompanying texts as it is clearly distinct from body copy.

Justified
Justified sees the text forced to fill out the line to both margins. This can allow the appearance of rivers of white space to appear and repeated hyphenation at the ends of lines if words are allowed to split. A designer must control the spacing and hyphenation to produce an attractive result.

Justified with last line aligned centre
This is an adapted justification method that sees the bulk of the text block justified so that the text lines fill out towards both right and left margins, while the last line is centred to produce a neat and attractive finish. This method is used for short pieces of text, such as pull quotes or introductory paragraphs.

Force justified
Force justified sees the text forced to fill out the line to the margins even if there are insufficient characters to do this naturally. It does this by introducing space between each character, which can make the text look uncomfortable. It is mainly used for headlines and subheads in editorial work.

Text can also be aligned along the vertical plane.

Top aligned
This alignment sees the text set from the top of the text box. Top aligned is the most commonly used setting.

Bottom aligned
This alignment sees the text set to the bottom of the text box leaving a space at the top.

Centre aligned
This alignment sees the text centrally set in the text box, with even spacing above and below.

Justified align

This alignment sees the text justified

throughout the height of the text box.

The setting of a text block can also combine vertical and horizontal alignment. For example, it can be justified in both dimensions or centred horizontally and bottom aligned.

see Hyphenation / Justification 136

SCREEN TERM

Aliasing

Anti-aliasing

A technique used to minimise the distortion artefacts (aliasing or so-called jaggies) that occur when something is converted to a lower resolution. Anti-aliasing is used with digital photography, text and computer graphics. Anti-aliasing removes those components that cannot be properly resolved when resampling to a lower resolution; in essence, it smoothes the jagged appearance of diagonal lines in a bitmapped image.

A designer has several choices in how to apply the technique: None, Sharp, Crisp, Strong and Smooth. The final result will depend on the colours, type size, font and so on, and some trial and error is necessary to achieve the desired finish.

see Jaggies 146

Back Edge

Also called spine edge

FINISHING TERM

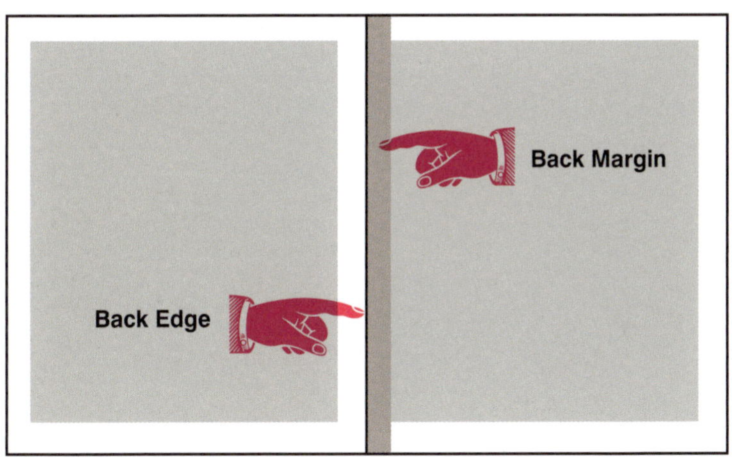

The part of a book block that is nearest to the spine. When bound, anything printed near the spine edge may be difficult to see. A designer needs to be aware of this lost space and compensate for it by leaving an appropriate back margin, as illustrated. The width of the back margin will depend on the binding type: some binding methods allow a book to fall open, while others do not.

see Book 41, Dummy 81

SCREEN TERM

The parts of a computer system, such as a website or design program, which consist of a user interface and the programming on which it operates. The front end is an interface that collects user input and processes it into a form that the back-end programming can use. A website user sees the front end and enters information or commands, which are processed by the back end to produce the desired result. The front end handles the look and feel of a site. The back end often includes databases and data-processing functions.

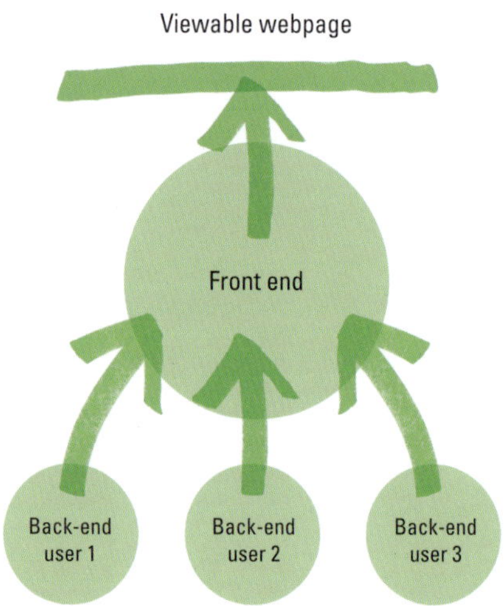

This diagram shows how the front-end and back-end concepts relate to each other.

DESIGN TERM

The hyphenation of words at the ends of the lines of a justified text block in such a way as to produce a poor visual result. The process of justifying text often breaks and hyphenates words so that the text adequately fills the line. When undertaken with little control, this can result in several consecutive hyphenated lines, which is visually poor from a design point of view, and can result in unsightly widows and orphans (single word lines at the end of a paragraph or the start of a column). Designers can exercise a great deal of control over a text block to correct bad breaks, which includes choosing where to break a word and adjusting the hyphenation settings to prevent consecutive line breaks. Kerning is used to adjust the spacing between words; letter spacing is used to adjust the spacing between letters.

see Hyphenation / Justification 136, Kerning 150, Orphans and Widows 180

PRINTING TERM

Banding is a series of lighter or darker bands or extraneous lines running across a print that are not part of the image. It may occur where one colour transitions to another, particularly where multiple passes are required to print each colour. Banding can occur with lithographic, inkjet, laser and other printing systems. There are several causes of banding particular to each printing system, but in general terms it can be reduced by adding a little noise to break up a pattern where banding occurs.

Banding may occur in multiple-pass printing where the page is not exactly lined up for each pass. The use of single-pass printers, which print all the colours in one pass, will resolve this issue. Banding may also occur with a coarse print resolution; in this case use a higher resolution. On inkjet printers, banding can occur when ink nozzles clog or the print heads are misaligned.

Banding can also occur when graduated tones are printed, such as on this page. This is because the colours are made from combinations of the four process colours that are deposited in a range of dot sizes produced by halftone screens.

A machine-readable representation of data. Developed by Bernard Silver in 1948–9, the barcode was inspired by Morse code with the dots and dashes extended into lines. There are different types of barcode: linear or 1D variations are made up of vertical, parallel lines and spaces; 2D matrix codes are patterns of squares, dots, hexagons and other geometric patterns. Different barcode systems include UPC (Universal Product Code) for retail and EAN (European Article Number) for magazines and books, as shown below.

UPC

EAN

DESIGN TERM

The basic structure that is used to guide the placement of type and graphic elements within a design. The baseline grid, when combined with text columns, provides a clear and definite method of handling type placement.

In this illustration, notice how the baseline grid allows for the cross-alignment of two different text blocks with different type size. This is achieved by ensuring the combined typesize and leading values are divisible. The main text block is set in 12-point type with 18 leading. The caption is set in 6-point type with 9 leading.

In this illustration , notice how the baseline grid allows for the cross-alignment of two different text blocks with different type size. This is achieved by ensuring the combined typesize and leading values are divisible. The main text block is set in 12-point type with 18 leading. The caption is set in 6-point type with 9 leading.

FINISHING TERM

A paper or plastic device that wraps around one or several copies of a publication. Bellybands, which can be a complete or partial loop, are so-named because they sit around the 'belly' of a publication like a belt. They serve a functional purpose of keeping documents together. Bellybands also have a decorative function by providing extra space for printing, for example on consumer magazines, where they inform readers of special offers or content. Pictured is a bellyband created by February Design; this clearly shows how it holds a publication closed.

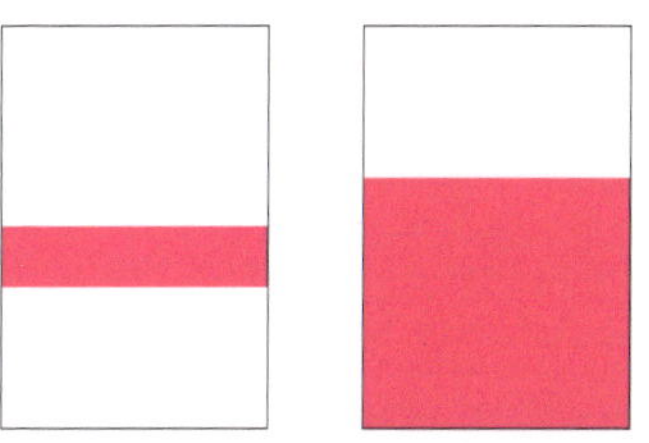

Bellybands are often thought of as being thin and narrow but they can be of any width, as this illustration shows.

DESIGN TERM

A proof correction mark used to indicate that type should be made bold. The weight of a particular typeface will be identified in its name, which is expressed in different ways for different type families. The Univers type family uses numbers to identify its different weights; other families use descriptive names such as heavy and bold, as shown.

Foundry Sans Bold

Univers 65 Black

Akzidenz Grotesk Super

Minion Semibold

News Gothic Condensed Bold

Gill Sans Ultra Bold

Franklin Gothic Heavy

see Font / Typeface 108, Proof Correction Marks 204

Also known as India paper

DESIGN TERM

A thin, lightweight, long-life, opaque paper grade typically made from 25% cotton and linen rags or flax with chemical wood pulp. Named after its most common usage, Bible paper allows for a higher number of pages within a given spine size compared to paper grades with higher bulk or caliper. As a high-quality, robust paper, it has many applications.

see Paper 187

FINISHING TERM

A print finishing process through which the pages of a publication are gathered and securely held together. There are many different types of binding, which have different durability, aesthetic, cost and functional characteristics, as shown here.

One key characteristic of binding methods is whether or not they allow pages to lie open flat. Where they do not, a designer should leave more space at the back edge or else it may be difficult to see the information printed.

Perfect binding
The backs of sections are removed and held together with a flexible adhesive, also used to attach a paper cover to the spine. The fore-edge is trimmed flat. Perfect binding is commonly used for paperback books.

Case binding
A common hard cover bookbinding method, also known as case binding. Signatures are sewn together, the spine is flattened, endsheets are added and headbands and tailbands are attached to the spine.

Spiral binding
A spiral of metal or plastic wire that winds through punched holes in the stock and allows the publication to open flat.

Wiro binding
A spine of metal (wiro) rings, which binds a document and allows it to open flat.

Comb binding
A spine of plastic (comb) rings, which binds a document and allows it to open flat.

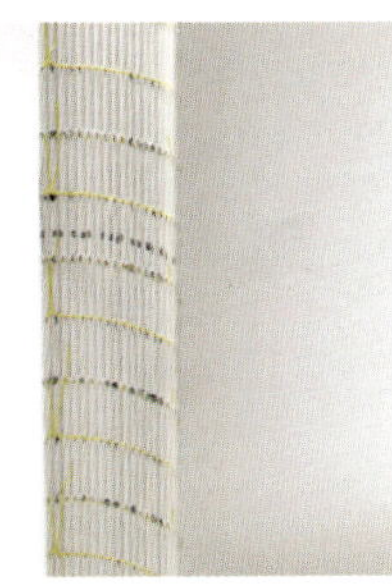

Open binding
A book bound without a cover to leave an exposed spine.

Canadian
A wiro-bound publication with a wraparound cover and an enclosed spine.

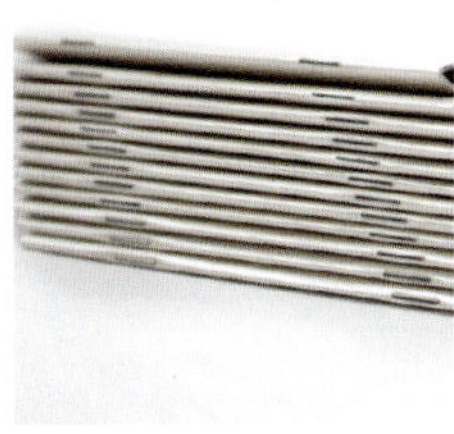

Saddle stitch
Signatures are nested and bound with wire stitches applied through the spine along the centrefold.

Clips and bolts
A fastening device that holds loose pages together. This usually requires a punched or drilled hole for the bolt or clip to pass through.

☛ see Canadian and Half Canadian Binding 48, Case Binding 51, Saddle Stitch 218

DESIGN TERM

Any graphic image that is composed of picture elements or pixels in a grid where each pixel contains colour information. Bitmap graphics have a fixed resolution, which means that when you resize them the image can become distorted and have a jagged, pixelated edge. Bitmaps are especially good for reproduction of detailed, tonal imagery and can easily be recoloured, such as the birds pictured here.

☛ see Jaggies 146, Pixel / Pixelation 195, Raster 208, Tonal Images 262

Also called floating black or translation black DESIGN TERM

The design contained on the black printing plate. Publications that are to be printed in several different languages are produced using the same cyan, magenta and yellow printing plates and a separate black printing plate for each language. This means that to print the publication in a different language only requires changing and proofing the one black plate, as shown here. Pictured below is a page printed in four colour (top) and how it appears on the black printer (bottom).

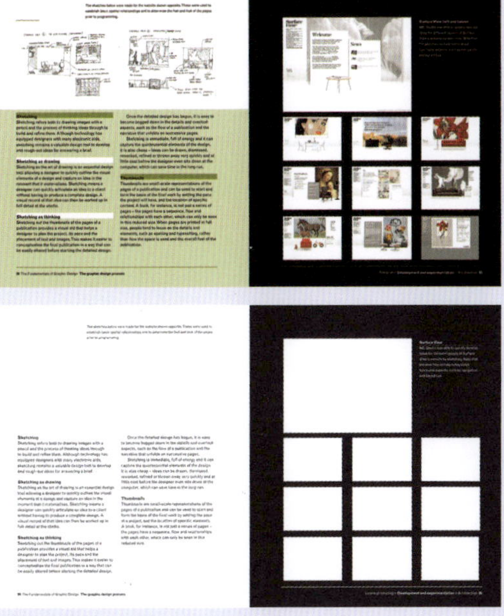

DESIGN TERM

Printed areas that extend beyond the 'trim', or the final finished size of the page. Without including a bleed, the printer will find it impossible to finish a job accurately and white edges will show where the pages are cut. Usually bleeds are set at 3mm, although more will be needed for some binding methods.

Pictured is *Into the Open*, a catalogue created by February Design for an exhibition by artists Ania Dabrowska and John Nassari at the Four Corners Gallery in London. The catalogue features text that bleeds off the page, with the intention of creating a tesselation with other copies of the same publication.

see Trim Marks 266

FINISHING TERM

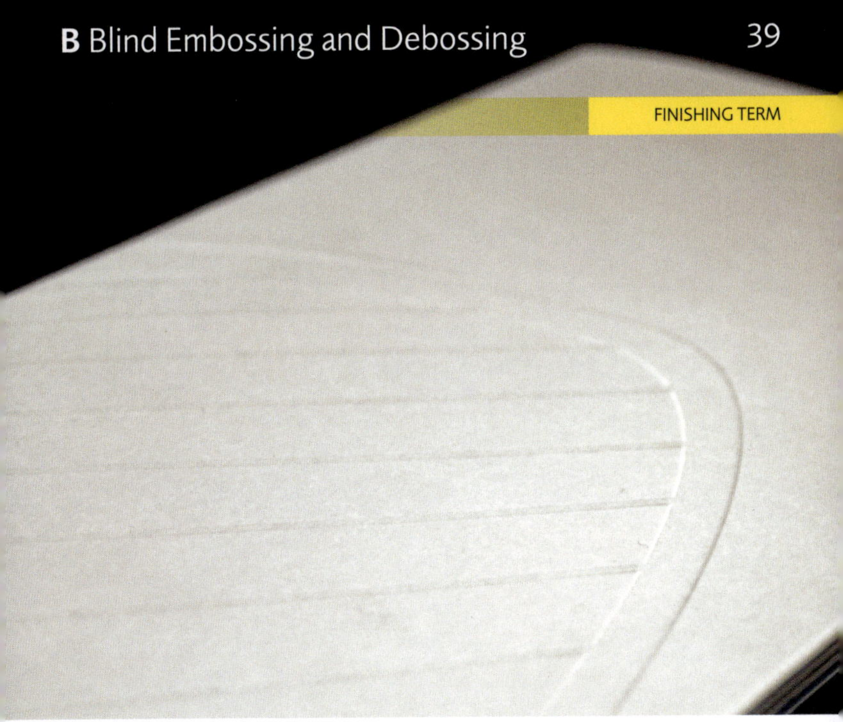

Pictured is a blind emboss cover created by To The Point for Evolvence Capital.

The process of stamping a metal die into a substrate to produce a decorative raised or indented surface. A blind emboss or deboss is essentially the naked impression left by the die in the substrate. An emboss may be made with foil to give colouration to the design, but they are frequently made blind – without the use of foil – to provide a tactile element.

☛ see Embossing and Debossing 87

PRINTING TERM

A paper-based substrate that is thicker and heavier than paper. Board generally has a grammage or weight over 224 GSM.

Flute or corrugated cardboard
A paper-based material consisting of a fluted corrugated sheet and one or two flat linerboards. Flute is used to produce corrugated boxes and other packing materials.

Millboard
A generic term for any solid paperboard that contains no cavities. Surfaces may be finished by couching or lining with an outer layer of higher grade materials. Millboard has a grammage of over 600 GSM and is used as a flat packaging material.

Grey board
A multi-use board, made entirely from waste paper, which may be lined or unlined.

Paperboard or cardboard
Used for packing and graphic printing, including book and magazine covers or postcards.

Fine board or hard board
A stiff, non-splitting paperboard with a hard surface, generally made from higher grades of waste paper, chemical pulp and textile waste. Fine board can be used for document covers.

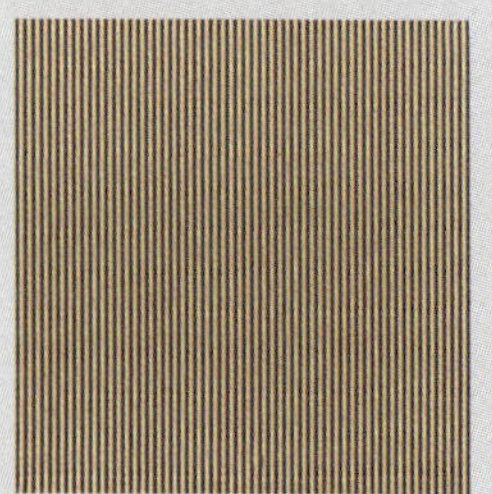

Flute or corrugated cardboard

Grey board

Cardboard

see GSM 122

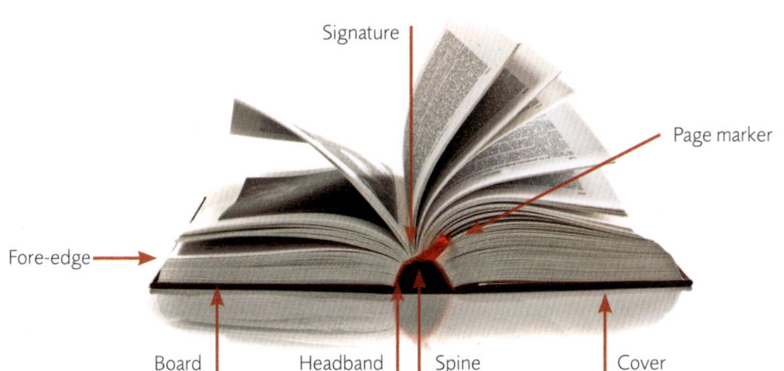

A set of printed pages that are fastened along one side and encased between protective covers. A book is typically comprised of a number of signatures, which are bound together using one of several different methods.

The anatomy of a book is made up of various parts that the designer can adjust and change. The boards, spine and cover material make up the case, which is created separately from the text block and attached to it. A dust jacket or slipcase is also created separately from the case and text block.

☛ see Dust Jacket 85, Page Marker 184, Signatures 234, Spine 240

FINISHING TERM

Materials typically used to cover hardcover books. The primary function of a book covering is to protect the book block and increase its life, but its visual appearance is also important. Bookcloth is the cheapest type of covering material and genuine leather the most expensive. Traditionally, books were sold as a book block, which the purchaser then bound according to their taste. Genuine leather was readily available and offered the greatest protection to what was considered a valuable asset. There are four main types of book finish:

Bookcloth: a material made from woven cotton or linen that gives a traditional, old-fashioned look.

Buckram: a highly durable, library-quality canvas, which is coated with vinyl so that it can be easily cleaned with a damp cloth.

Genuine leather: a covering made from real leather.

Bonded leather: a material made with leather fibres that are bonded together with an adhesive, such as latex, and finished to look similar to genuine leather.

Pictured are swatches of bookcloth that will be used to select the colour of a hardcover book.

A navigation system for websites. There are three types of web breadcrumbs: path, location and attribute. Path breadcrumbs are dynamic and show the exact route that a user has taken to arrive at a given webpage. Location breadcrumbs are static and simply show where a page is located in a website hierarchy. Attribute breadcrumbs give information that categorises the current page. Breadcrumb is sometimes incorrectly called cookie crumb, which is actually an HTTP cookie file. The term comes from the trail of breadcrumbs left by Hansel and Gretel in the fairytale.

Book Page Page This page

Path breadcrumb

A breadcrumb that shows where you are and how you entered the site. People do not always enter a website through the homepage; they may perhaps use a search engine to enter on a specific page. The breadcrumb bar here shows how you arrived at this page, in this book.

Book Chapter This page

Location breadcrumb

A breadcrumb that shows where you are in the hierarchy of a website, irrespective of where you entered it. The bar above is a breadcrumb for this book. Here it states that you are in a book, then in a chapter and then in a page.

This page tells you about...breadcrumbs

Attribute breadcrumb

A breadcrumb that tells you about the specific page you are visiting.

DESIGN TERM

The volume of light reflected off a sheet of paper, rated on a scale of 0–100: the higher the number, the brighter the sheet. Typical white papers range from 80 to 95. High brightness is essential for achieving a superior image quality. Brightness is not the same as whiteness, which is the quality of light; it refers to the shade of the sheet of paper. However, most papers are manufactured to a blue-white shade because, to the human eye, this shade appears to be brighter.

Brightness also refers to a photo-editing tool that allows you to change the contrast in an image.

Image contrast can be increased by using the brightness command (above).

Paper brightness is typically in the range of 80 to 95 (left).

see Paper 187, Stock 246

B Bulk

Also known as thickness or caliper PRINTING TERM

The thickness of a sheet of paper. Generally speaking, paper with higher basis weight, as measured in GSM, has greater bulk, but there are exceptions. Some stocks are made to have greater bulk but without the weight gain. Stock with greater bulk tends to feel more substantial between the fingers than typical printing paper. Printers can make a bulking dummy using unprinted sheets of stock so that a designer can see and feel what the weight of a publication will be like.

see Dummy 81, GSM 122

SCREEN TERM

A clickable graphic device that represents a link to a page or piece of content on a webpage or other digital media. Buttons are used for navigating a website; they give a user the means to access different pages, return to the homepage or go back to a previously visited page. A button has three states: off, hover and on. Off is the button's normal state. The hover state typically sees a change of colour when the cursor is rolled over it to allow people to see that it is a button. On may see the button seem to depress as it is clicked to activate the link. Buttons are often graphic icons, which need to be simple enough to understand and visually interesting to attract attention.

B Button and String

FINISHING TERM

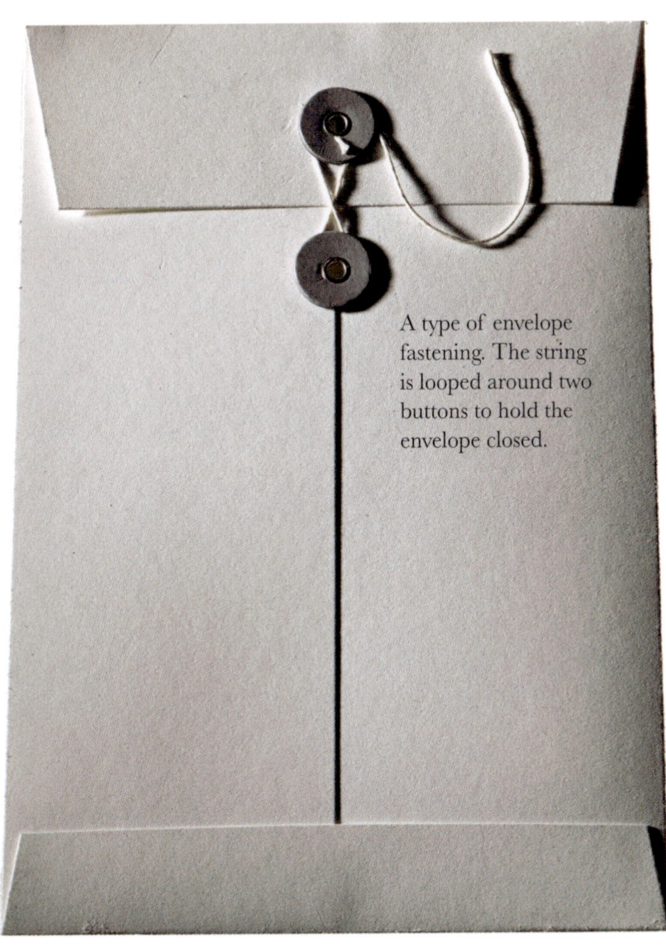

A type of envelope fastening. The string is looped around two buttons to hold the envelope closed.

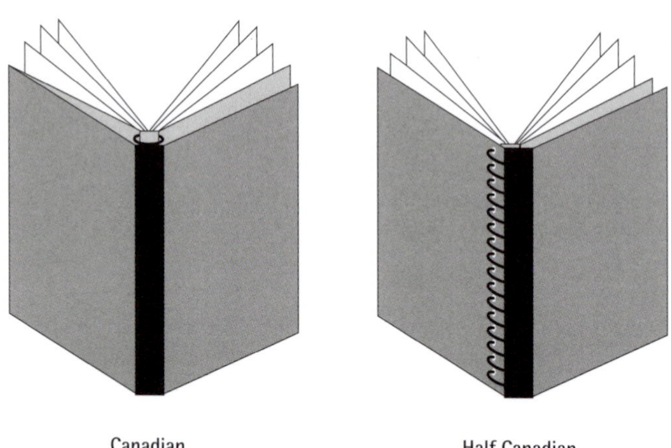

Canadian

Half Canadian

Canadian

A wiro-bound publication with a full wraparound cover and an enclosed spine. This binding allows the pages of the publication to lie flat, with the wiro fixings hidden.

Half Canadian

A wiro-bound publication with a partial wraparound cover and an exposed spine. This binding allows the pages of the publication to lie flat, with the wiro fixings partially exposed.

see Binding 34, Spine 240

SCREEN TERM

Original image
This is the original image, which is a certain size.

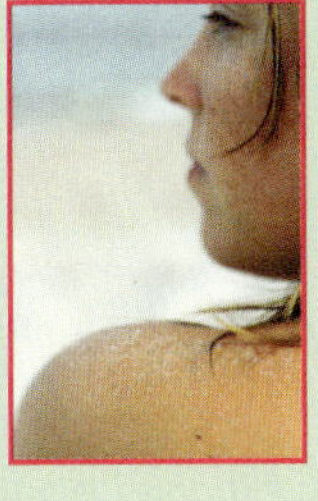

Altering image size
Altering the image size changes its height and width.

Altering canvas size
Altering the canvas size changes the size of the 'board' the image is on. When the canvas size is made bigger than the image (as shown), the space can be filled with background colour. If made smaller, the image will be cropped.

The overall size of the working space available in an image-editing program, irrespective of its contents. Images, which can be resized independently, are placed on the 'canvas' to be worked upon. Altering the size of the canvas does not change image size, although it may crop the image or increase the amount of space surrounding it.

see Crop 69, Resolution 213

SCREEN TERM

A style sheet language that describes the presentation and formatting of a document written in a website markup language, such as HTML and XHTML. In general, CSS means that the page creator's style sheet takes precedence over that of the browser designer or the viewer. CSS allows the separation of document content from document presentation, which can improve content accessibility, provide more flexibility and control the specification of presentation characteristics.

Look at the source code for a webpage, below, to see how CSS can be used to control the representation of text.

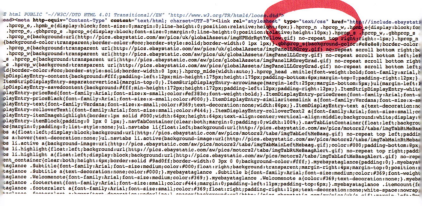

```
E html PUBLIC "-//W3C//DTD HTML 4.01 Transitional//EN" "http://www.w3.org/TR/html4/loose.dtd">
ead><meta http-equiv="Content-Type" content="text/html; charset=UTF-8"><link rel="stylesheet" type="text/css" href="http://include.ebaystati
 .hprcp_e,.hpmb_e{display:block;font-size:0;margin:0;line-height:0;position:relative;height:6px;}.hprcp_n .hprcp_w,.hpmb_e{display:block;fo
 .hprcp_e,.gbhprcp_s .hprcp_e{display:block;font-size:0;margin:0;line-height:0;position:relative;height:10px;}.hprcp_s .hprcp_w,.gbhprcp_s
 .hprcp_e{background:url(http://pics.ebaystatic.com/aw/pics/uk/globalAssets/imgHPHdrRgtYellow.gif) no-repeat top right;right:-1px;}.hprcp_n
{background-color:transparent;border-color:#ccc;border-style:solid;border-width:0 1px 1px;}.gbhprcp_s{background-color:#e8e8e8;border-color
 .hprcp_e{background:transparent url(http://pics.ebaystatic.com/aw/pics/uk/globalAssets/imgPanelLRGrey.gif) no-repeat scroll bottom right;b
 .hprcp_w{background:transparent url(http://pics.ebaystatic.com/aw/pics/uk/globalAssets/imgPanelLLGrey.gif) no-repeat scroll bottom left;le
_s .hprcp_e{background:transparent url(http://pics.ebaystatic.com/aw/pics/globalAssets/imgPanelLRGreyGrad.gif) no-repeat scroll bottom right
_s .hprcp_w{background:transparent url(http://pics.ebaystatic.com/aw/pics/globalAssets/imgPanelLLGreyGrad.gif) no-repeat scroll bottom left;
id{border-color:#ccc;border-style:solid;border-width:0 1px;}.hprcp_mide{width:auto;}.hprcp_head .mtitle{font-weight:bold;font-family:arial,
ipDisplayEntry-content{background:#fff;padding-left:12px;min-height:175px;height:175px;padding-bottom:6px;margin-top:0;padding-right:12px;}
ItemStripDisplayEntry-separatorvertical{margin-top:0;}.ItemStripDisplayEntry-arrowimage{margin-left:25px;margin-bottom:5px;}ul{margin-left:
ipDisplayEntry-savedcontent{background:#fff;min-height:172px;height:172px;padding-left:12px;padding-right:12px;}.ItemStripDisplayEntry-white
playEntry-priceRed{font-family:Arial;font-size:x-small;color:#ef383c;font-weight:bold;}.ItemDisplayEntry-priceGreen{font-family:Arial;font-
playEntry-priceBlack{font-family:Arial;font-size:x-small;color:#000;}.ItemDisplayEntry-similaritemslink a{font-family:Verdana;font-size:x-s
playEntry-text{font-family:Verdana;font-size:x-small;color:#369;text-decoration:none;width:86px;}.ItemDisplayEntry-text a{text-decoration:n
playEntry-rolloverText1{font-family:Arial;font-size:small;color:#444;}.ItemDisplayEntry-rolloverText2 a{font-family:Arial;font-size:small;c
playEntry-itemImagehighlight{border:1px solid #000;width:64px;height:64px;text-align:center;vertical-align:middle;background:white;display:
playEntry-itemBlock{padding:0 1px 0 1px;}.navTabContainer{clear:both;margin:0;padding:0;width:100%;}.navTabListContainer{float:left;backgro
bs{margin:0;padding:0;list-style:none;}ul.navtabs li{float:left;background:url(http://pics.ebaystatic.com/aw/pics/motors2/tabs/imgTabRtMeBa
bs a{float:left;display:block;background:url(http://pics.ebaystatic.com/aw/pics/motors2/tabs/imgTabLeftMeBaag.gif) no-repeat top left;paddi
bs a:hover{text-decoration:none;}ul.navtabs li.active{background-image:url(http://pics.ebaystatic.com/aw/pics/motors2/tabs/imgTabMainRtMeba
bs li.active a{background-image:url(http://pics.ebaystatic.com/aw/pics/motors2/tabs/imgTabMainLeftMebaag.gif);color:#000;padding-bottom:8px
bs li.highlight{float:left;background:url(http://pics.ebaystatic.com/aw/pics/motors2/tabs/imgTabRtMeBaagAlert.gif) no-repeat top right;padd
bs li.highlight a{float:left;display:block;background:url(http://pics.ebaystatic.com/aw/pics/motors2/tabs/imgTabLeftMeBaagAlert.gif) no-rep
ent_container{clear:both;height:4px;border:solid #9ad0ff;border-width:0 3px 0 0;background-color:#fff;}.myebayataglance{padding:0;}.myebaya
taglance .Subtitle{font-family:Arial;font-size:medium;color:#000;float:right;background:transparent;margin-right:4px;margin-top:0;position:
taglance .Subtitle a{text-decoration:none;color:#000;}.myebayataglance .Subtitle b{font-family:Arial;font-size:medium;color:#369;font-weight
taglance .Welcomenote{font-family:Arial;font-size:medium;color:#369;}.myebayataglance .Welcomenote a{color:#369;text-decoration:none;}.myeb
taglance .footertext{font-family:Arial;font-size:small;color:#444;margin:0;padding-left:11px;padding-top:6px;}.myebayataglance .itemcount{f
taglance .footeralert a{font-family:Arial;font-size:small;color:#369;float:right;padding-right:11px;text-decoration:none;white-space:nowrap;
```

see HTML 133

FINISHING TERM

A common hard-cover bookbinding method. The technique involves sewing signatures together, flattening the spine, applying endsheets and attaching headbands and tailbands to the spine. Hard covers are attached, the spine is usually rounded and grooves along the cover edge act as hinges.

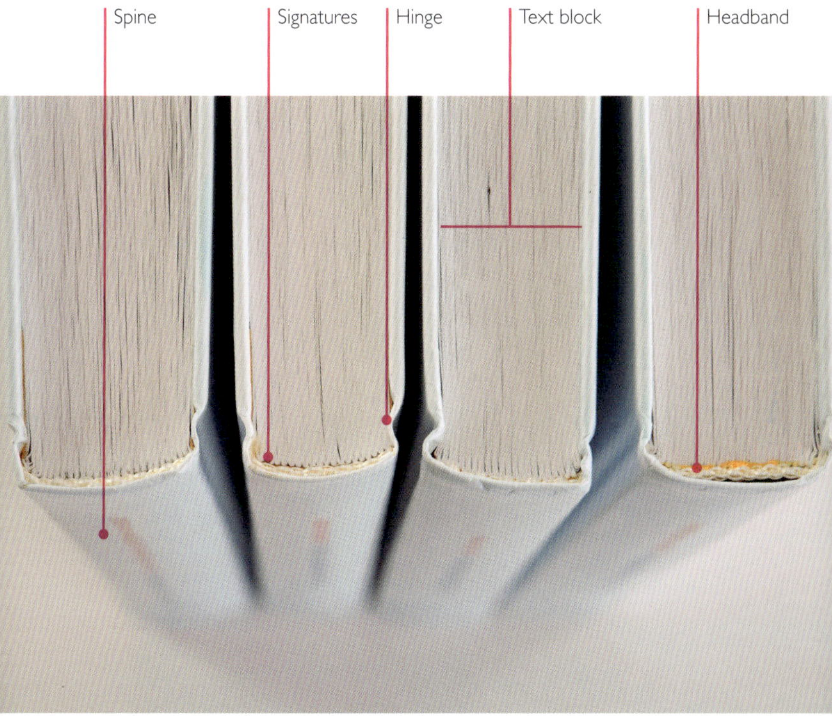

see Binding 34, Book 41, Endpapers 89, Headband / Tailband 129, Spine 240

DESIGN TERM

The stored colour information of a digital image. Each digital image contains different channels that store information for the different colours of its colour space. The common colour spaces are RGB and CMYK. RGB images are made from the red, green and blue additive primaries and have three channels, one for each colour, as illustrated. CMYK images are made from the cyan, magenta, yellow and black subtractive primaries and have four channels, one for each colour. An image stored as RGB is smaller than a CMYK file because it has one channel fewer. For this reason, RGB images are typically used for web or digital media applications. CYMK images are used for printing with the four-colour printing process, as each channel corresponds to one of the printing plates. A digital image can be split so that each of its channels can be worked on and adjusted individually.

see CMYK 54, RGB 216

DESIGN TERM

Clone stamp
The clone stamp tool appears like a rubber stamp in the toolbar.

Uses
The clone stamp easily samples the blue sky to seamlessly remove the aeroplane.

A tool that is used to sample parts of an image and apply them to a specific area; it is typically used to remove an image element. The clone stamp tool works particularly well in flat-textured areas, such as the sky in this image, in which the aircraft has been removed. It is more complex using the clone tool where there is colour graduation as it can result in obvious pattern repetition, although this can be reduced by careful use of a defocus filter, such as averaging.

see Filters 96, Image Manipulation 138

PRINTING TERM

The four subtractive primary process colours used to reproduce colour images in the four-colour printing process. Cyan, magenta and yellow are subtractive primaries that are combined in printing to make the additive primaries (red, green and blue) of visible light that we see.

Different colours can be created by mixing these process colours in different concentrations or percentages. However, there are limitations and some colour combinations do not work. Anything too light may not be clear due to the limitations of the printing process. Mixes where the combined percentage of the different colours is above 260 may result in a murky, muddy colour, as shown in the third chip below. Using a Pantone colour book can help a designer to select colour combinations that will print as desired.

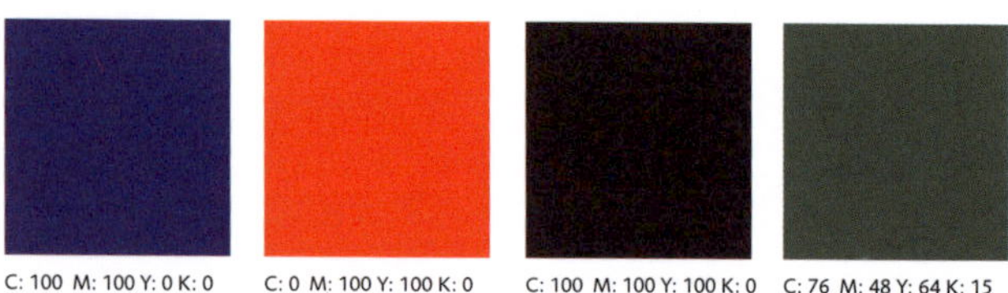

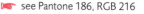

see Pantone 186, RGB 216

A distortion of paper stock that appears as a ripple or wave, caused by changes in humidity during transportation and storage and/or the introduction of moisture to the stock. Named after the wave form of a cockle shell, cockling causes print problems on the press and makes it difficult to print in registration. Paper stock is typically stored for at least a couple of days at the print shop prior to use so that it can acclimatise to the ambient humidity, as shown below.

☞ see Paper 187, Stock 246

DESIGN TERM

The adjustment of the colour space of a monitor or other piece of equipment to a given standard. For example, sRGB or standard RGB is a device-independent calibrated colour space, which was defined by HP and Microsoft in the 1990s to provide a consistent way to display colour internet images on computer screens (CRTs). It is essential that both the monitor and the output devices that print colour proofs are calibrated to ensure accurate colour reproduction on the printed page. Colour calibration of a monitor can be achieved using a tool such as a Spyder to give consistent and accurate colour response.

Colorimeter
An instrument used in colorimetry to profile and calibrate output devices.

Spectrometer
An instrument used to measure properties of light of a printed piece. A spectrometer scans and measures the colour bar on printed sheets, converting the results to numeric data, which allows colour adjustments to be made. Spectrometers measure solid densities, dot gain, trapping, contrast, hue error and greyness.

see Dot Gain / Dot Size 78, RGB 216

The specification of a print job that includes information about colour usage.

For a simple job, such as a flyer for instance, one side might print 4 colour, with the reverse printing black only. This would be expressed as 4/1, or 4 back 1 (as shown below). If it printed 5 colour one side, and 3 on the reverse then it would be expressed as 5 back 3 and so on.

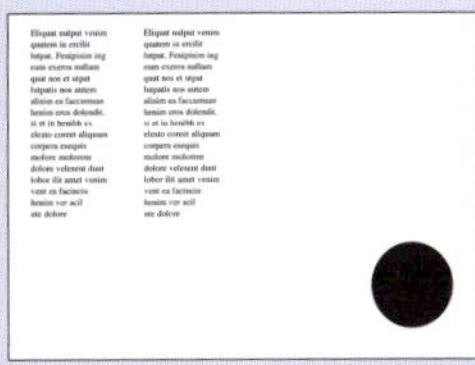

4/1 or four colours on one side, one colour on the other.

A more complicated job might involve a more in-depth plan for colour fall. In a book of 32 pages for example, pages 1, 4, 5, 8, 9, 12, 13 and 16 of the first signature would print on one side, with the remaining pages on the reverse. Its colour plan would look like the diagram below. A colour fall plan needs to be produced in conjunction with a printer, because it depends on press size, number of pages to view, and whether the job is work and turn or work and tumble.

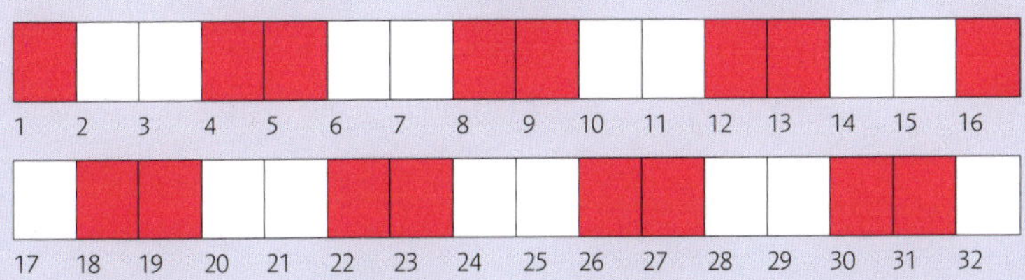

see Imposition 139, Signatures 234, Work and Tumble / Turn 256

DESIGN TERM

A vertical structure that contains and organises body text on a page. A page may have one or several text columns and they can be of any width; it depends on the number of text elements to be presented and the number of characters they contain. For example, a magazine spread may contain an extended article that is either one continuous body of text or several short and unrelated items. The use of columns automatically creates a gutter or a space between them. A designer can control the gutter size, making it wider or thinner, enabling the text to be read easily.

If the gutter between columns is too tight, the words from one column appear to run into the next one. As a consequence, a reader may mistakenly read across adjacent columns as it is not obvious where a line ends. In addition, it will make it more difficult for the eye to locate the start of each line on the second and subsequent columns.

If the gutter is too wide, the text in the columns appears to be unrelated and will seem like unlinked text blocks. This makes it more difficult for the eye to jump from one column to the next.

see Gutter 124

Composite

An element made up from distinct components. In graphic design, the final image is often a composite of many components such as text, photos and illustrations. The printing process can add further components such as stock, varnish, emboss and foil block.

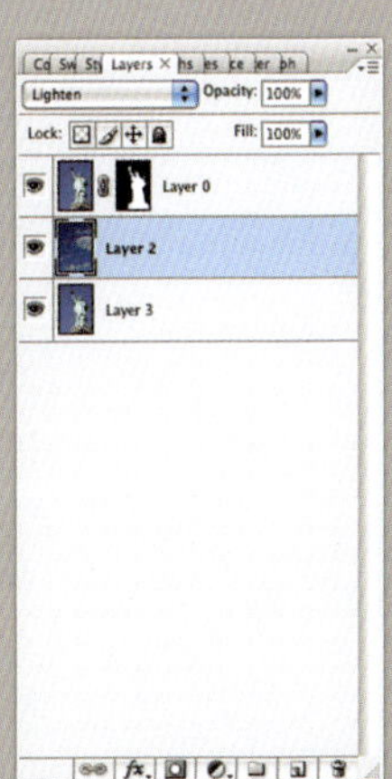

The toolbox (above) shows the different layers used to create the composite image (left).

see Layers 155

DESIGN TERM

One of various processes that reduces the information contained within a digital file and therefore reduces it in size. Compression can be lossy or lossless. Lossy compression methods, such as JPEG, discard information, which can result in image degradation via the appearance of compression artefacts or jaggies (above right). Lossy methods are typically used for photographic images where loss of fidelity is acceptable. Lossless compression produces no visible deterioration in image quality and results in a clear image (above left). These methods include TIFF, BMP and GIF.

see GIF 115, Jaggies 146, JPEG 148, TIFF 259

SCREEN TERM

Computer technology that is used to design and model objects in two or three dimensions. CAD allows a designer to draft precise shapes and include technical information such as materials, processes, dimensions and tolerances according to specific regulations or conventions. CAD is used to design building interiors and exteriors, exhibition stands and objects. Pictured is a housing design created by Nick Beard at TEAM Homes, which illustrates the power of CAD. The 3D image can be rotated to any viewing angle to give a clear appreciation and representation of the design.

C Computer to Plate (CTP)

PRINTING TERM

Imaging technology used in printing whereby a design is output directly on to a printing plate. Traditional printing methods see a design output on to film, which is then used to make a printing plate. Computer-to-plate technology is a quicker and cheaper method for making printing plates, and a sharper and more detailed image is transferred, with reduced risk of registration problems. Pictured is an operator loading a plate into a VLF CTP system.

see Plate 196, Printing 200, Registration 211

C Concertina

Also known as accordion fold

FINISHING TERM

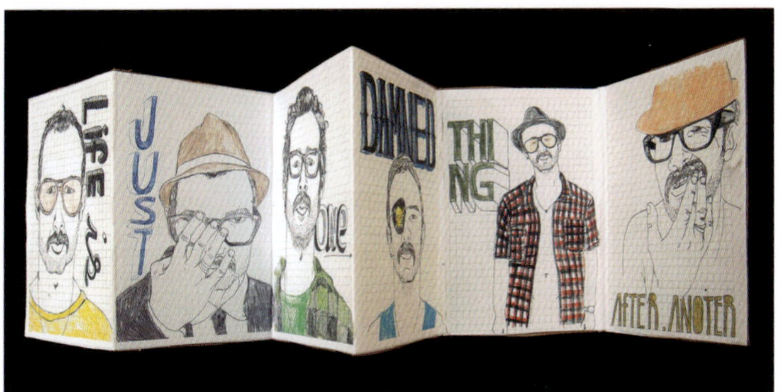

A series of parallel folds, so-named because its shape resembles the bellows of a concertina. A concertina fold requires that the outer page panel is larger than the inner page panels in order to conceal the folding edges of the final piece, as shown below. Alternatively, a concertina can be folded in on itself by making the page panels incrementally smaller. The bulk of the stock will affect the measurement of the page panels so that they nest comfortably. Pictured is a design created by Amée Christian, which features a concertina of five folds.

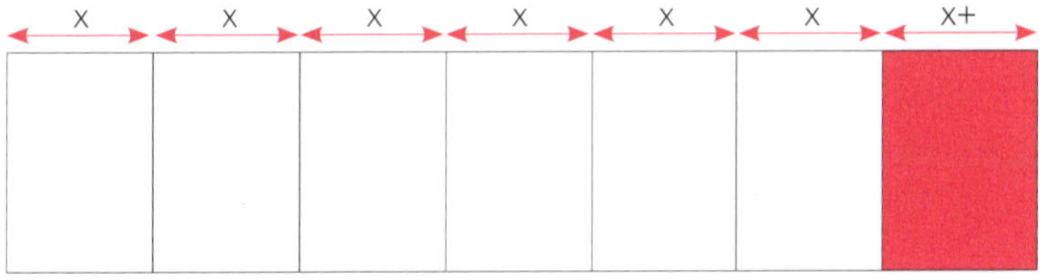

see Bulk 45, Folding 106, Stock 246

DESIGN TERM

Narrow and wide versions of a roman typeface. Condensed typefaces are useful for tight spaces, while extended types are often used for headlines to dramatically fill a space. Condensed and extended typefaces are often available in different weight variations, from light through to black, to give further typesetting flexibility. **Typographer Adrian Frutiger developed a type numbering system for the Univers type family in 1957, which identifies the width and weight of each member of the family. In any two-digit number the first digit, or designator, refers to the line weight; this ranges from 2, the thinnest, to 9, the widest. The second digit refers to the character width, with 3 being the most extended and 9 being the most condensed. If the second number is even it indicates an italic face, while odd numbers represent a roman face. This numbering system was designed to eliminate the confusion caused by different naming systems such as thin, black, heavy and so on.**

CONDENSED

27 Ultra Light Condensed

EXTENDED

93 Black Extended

see Font / Typeface 108, Weight 284

An image where the colour at any given point is produced as a single tone, such as for black-and-white and colour photographs. The four-colour offset lithography printing process uses screens to convert a continuous tone image into a series of halftone dots. As such, the resulting reproduced image no longer has continuous tone.

see Halftone 126

DESIGN TERM

The difference between the highlights and the shadows of an image. Contrast is the level of tone separation from white to black. High contrast can help make images clearer, as shown below. It can also make text more readable. Notice how the thin strokes and uniform stroke weight of the first alphabet below results in low contrast, making it more difficult to read than the middle example. Too much contrast can make typefaces difficult to read, as the bottom alphabet illustrates.

ABCDEFGHIJKLMNOPQRSTUVWXYZ

ABCDEFGHIJKLMNOPQRSTUVWXYZ

ABCDEFGHIJKLMNOPQRSTUVWXYZ

see Font / Typeface 108

DESIGN TERM

A set of two or more numbers that are used to determine the position of a point, line, curve, plane or element in a space with a given dimension. Coordinates are represented by the letters x and y, where x refers to the horizontal and y to the vertical addresses of the point in question. Coordinates may refer to absolute scales such as millimetres or pixels and they are used in several different instances in pre-press. Layout programs allow designers to specify exact coordinates, positioning design elements with greater accuracy than is possible by eye alone. Coordinates are also used when drawing curves and graphs. In web applications, each clickable area of an image map is specified by a pair of x and y coordinates relative to the upper left-hand corner of the image.

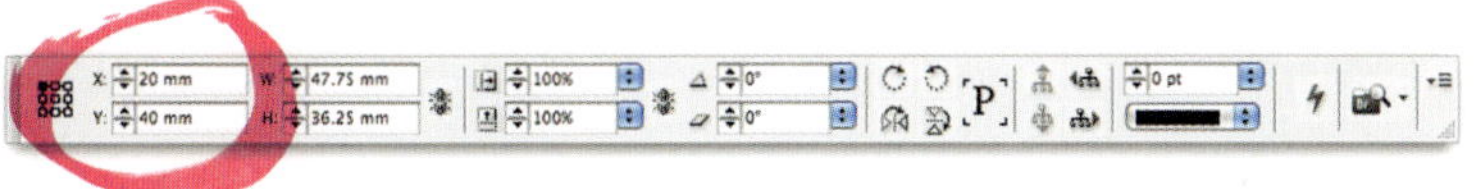

Pictured is a tool bar from a design layout program; the highlighted section shows the anchor coordinates of an item.

X refers to the horizontal address of a point.

Y refers to the vertical address of a point.

FINISHING TERM

The occurrence of inner folded pages of a publication (or printed section) extending further than the outer folded pages. It is usually caused by the bulk of the paper or the extent of the publication. Creep may not be a problem in saddle-stitched publications that are untrimmed, but information near the trim edge in perfect-bound publications may be lost, so design elements need to be positioned away from the fore-edge.

The fold helps the leaves of the publication slot together.

The greater the number of leaves, the greater the creep as the fore-edge of the centre pages is forced out past the outer pages.

see Bulk 45, Dummy 81, Saddle Stitch 218

DESIGN TERM

To cut or trim part of a photograph or picture. Cropping typically involves the reduction of the outer boundaries of the image to focus the attention on its main subject, or to increase its dynamic tension. The close crop on the image below helps place the model's face at the centre of attention. Cropping is often undertaken in conjunction with graphic methods such as the rule of thirds, as shown below.

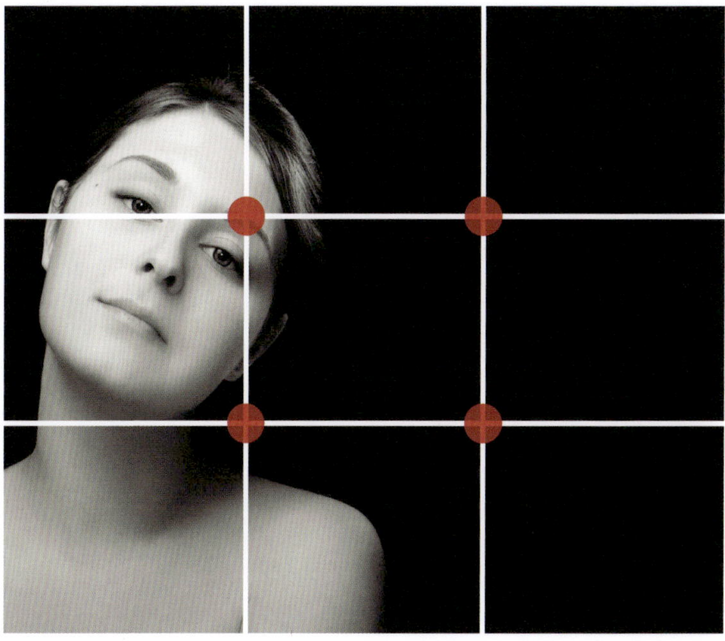

PRINTING TERM

An instrument that precisely measures the density of colour on a printed image to determine if the printing was consistent throughout the run. A densitometer is used to check colour saturation and to calibrate printing equipment. Densitometers are often used when press passing to ensure that the printed piece is an accurate reproduction of the match print. A densitometer takes a reading from the solid blocks of colour printed on the side of a sheet and/or match print (shown above).

☛ see Colour Calibration 56, Proofs 206, Striker Bar 248

The removal of colour that leaves the tonal values of an image intact. A designer can desaturate an entire image, which effectively sees it assimilate a greyscale image, or certain image areas can be masked. The model has been masked in the images below so that the background can be desaturated.

The original image features a prominent element in the shape of the red coat.

Here, the model is masked and the background desaturated to 70%. Notice how the unmasked areas begin to stand out.

Full desaturation sees the background completely desaturated, focusing attention on the model.

Masks
A utilitarian layer in a photo-editing program, which protects parts of an image while others are being worked on. Importantly, the mask and image are separate so if a mistake is made on the mask, the original image remains intact.

see Selective Colour 225

DESIGN TERM

A photo-editing filter that removes visual interference from a digital image to improve quality. Despeckle can be used to blur the pixels where there is a significant shift in brightness, smoothing out any visual interference, such as moiré, while preserving detail. It can also be used to reduce noise in an image, such as salt-and-pepper noise (dark and white spots of pixels that are a different colour or intensity from surrounding pixels), which may be caused by dust in the camera. However, despeckle cannot correct a very poor original image.

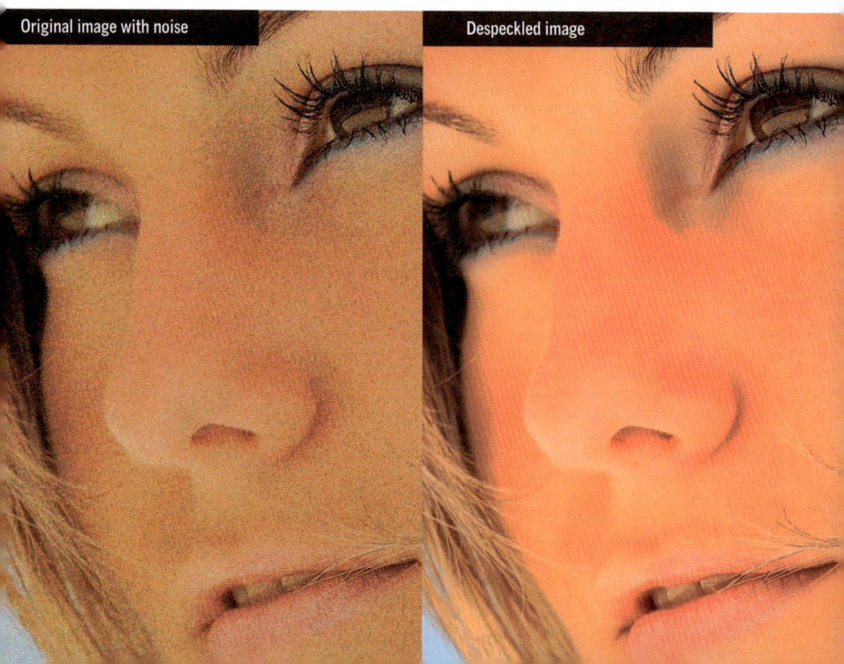
Original image with noise

Despeckled image

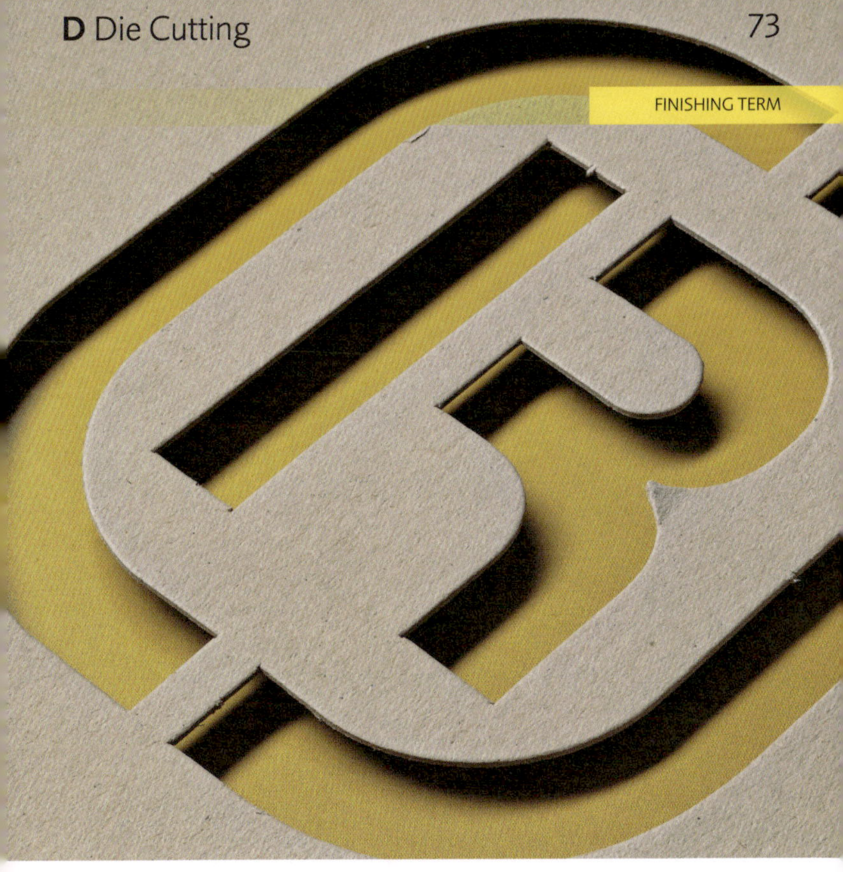

The removal of parts of a design using a metal die. When specifying a die cut you need to ensure that areas don't become isolated and fall out. The above example is a Research Studios brochure; it features their logo, which has been die cut. Notice how small arms have been left to contain the inner circle of the design.

FINISHING TERM

A foil with a holographic pattern that diffracts light to create a rainbow effect. It can be used with a custom-engraved tool to create a low-cost hologram on printed products such as tickets (see more on holograms on page 132). Diffraction foils are available in a range of patterns and colours. The example below, by Miha Artnak, shows the unique quality of these foils.

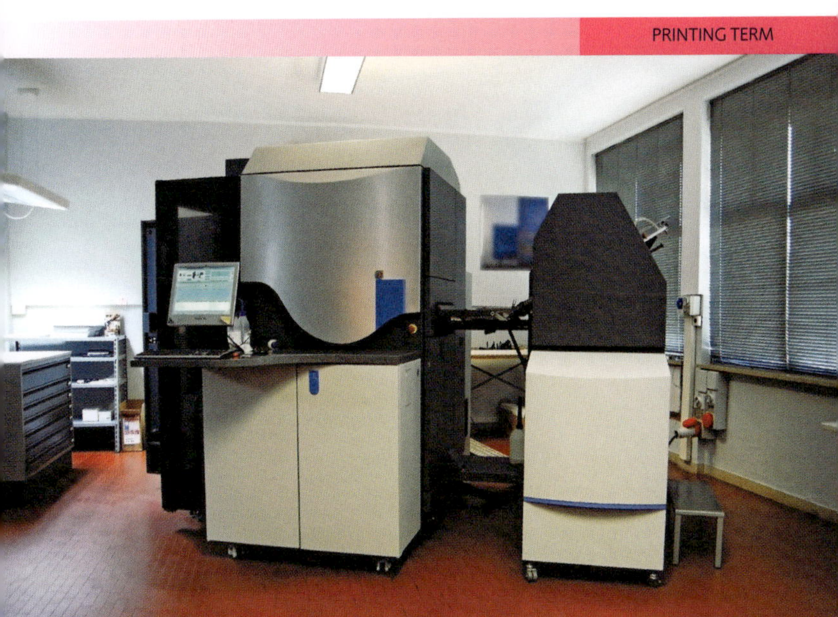

The reproduction of digital material on a physical surface without the use of printing plates. Digital printing is a highly flexible method that differs from traditional printing techniques, such as lithography, flexography, gravure and letterpress, in that every print can be altered and made different. As such, digital printing is appropriate for short print runs and the customisation of content or variable data printing (VDP). Compared with traditional methods, there is less chemical usage and paper waste, the ink is not absorbed by the substrate and setup times are quicker. A range of different substrates are available for use with digital printers, including uncoated and recycled stocks.

☛ see Printing 200, Stock 246, Substrate 251, Variable Data Printing 272

FINISHING TERM

A standard stationery size used for business envelopes and compliments slips throughout the world, except in the US and Canada. The DL size, which is about a third of the size of A4, falls out of the ISO system and equipment manufacturers have complained that it is slightly too small for reliable automatic enveloping. As such, the C6/C5 envelope format was developed as an alternative.

These envelopes were created by Frost Design for ADG.

☛ see ISO 145, A Sizes 290, B Sizes 291, C Sizes 293

Dodge and Burn

The eyes, lips and hair of the model (right) have been burned to bring more contrast to the image.

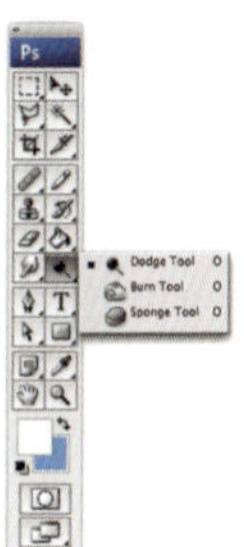

A tool used to lighten or darken areas of an image, which replicates traditional photographic exposure-regulating techniques on specific print areas. Dodging holds back light to lighten an area while burning increases exposure to darken print areas. The dodge-and-burn tool features various options that allow you to change midtone, shadow and highlight areas. The tool can be used as an airbrush.

see Retouching 214

PRINTING TERM

When printing, the aim is to produce a halftone dot that is as circular as possible in order to reproduce a clear image. More porous stocks cause the ink to spread, which means the image may lose definition.

A printing problem that sees the spreading and enlarging of ink dots on the stock during printing. Dot gain may be a particular problem with stocks that are more absorbent because the ink spreads out as it soaks into the paper. Dot gain is checked during the printing process by reviewing the star target on the striker bar printed at the edge of the sheet. Dot size is determined by the halftone screens that are used to make the colour separations for a print job using the process colours.

☛ see Halftone 126

DESIGN TERM

DPI (dots per inch) refers to the number of dots produced by a printer. For example, in lithography, 300dpi is standard. When a printer requests an image at a certain dpi, they actually mean ppi (see below).

PPI (pixels per inch) is a reference to the number of pixels (displayed vertically and horizontally) in each square inch of a digital image. This reflects how much information an image contains. For example, a 300ppi image contains nine times more information than a 100ppi image.
This is often referred to as dpi, but a digital image is made of pixels, not dots.

LPI (lines per inch) is a measure of detail in a printed halftone image. Put simply, the more lines per inch, the tighter the configuration of dots and the smoother the image. On porous stocks such as newsprint, for example, a low lpi (around 85lpi) is used to prevent colour bleeding.

SPI (samples per inch) is a measure of resolution for a scanner or camera.
This is also often referred to as dpi, but a scanner doesn't print dots.

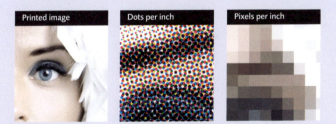

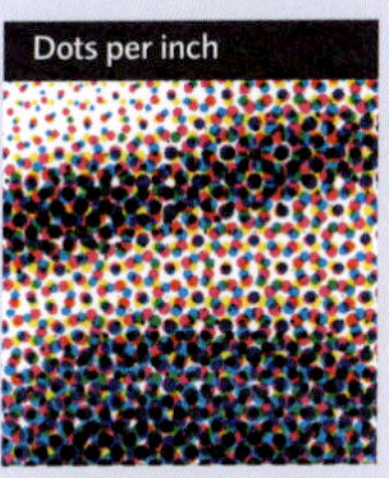

If you look closely, the printed image is made of individual printed dots: dpi. The original is a digital image, made of pixels: ppi. The capture of the image, whether it be by camera or scanner, involves spi. And finally, when deciding how to print it – ie, on coarse or fine stock – lpi needs to be considered.

☛ see Halftone 126, Newsprint 174, Resolution 213

SCREEN TERM

A web development software program created by Macromedia and now developed by Adobe Systems. Using a WYSIWYG (pronounced wisiwig) interface, Dreamweaver allows non-technical people to create webpages. Available for both Mac and Windows, Dreamweaver supports a range of web technologies including CSS and JavaScript.

W What
Y You
S See
I Is
W What
Y You
G Get

see Cascading Style Sheets (CSS) 50

PRINTING TERM

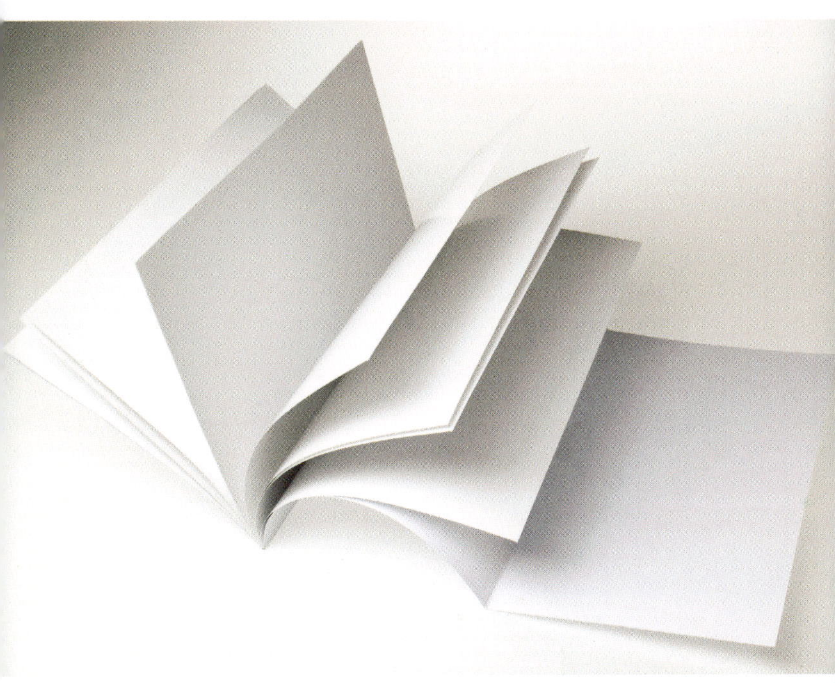

Prototype of a publication in the chosen stock. A dummy enables the designer to get a feel for the publication: its weight, its bulk, the size of its spine and how the stock creeps when bound in signatures.

see Bulk 45, Signatures 234, Spine 240, Stock 246

DESIGN TERM

Pictured is a spread created by NB Studio, which features a duotone used to homogenise different photographic images by giving them the same treatment.

A tonal image created using two different colours, one of which is typically black. In a duotone image, the white values are essentially replaced with the secondary colour. Each colour can be altered independently for subtle results (see opposite, top) or something more graphic (see opposite, bottom); here the secondary colour has been flooded, creating an effect similar to screening the black on to a solid colour base.

A duotone is created using two colours. In the example here, black and yellow are used to colour the image. Everything that was white in the original image becomes a shade of yellow, while the blacks remain as they were.

Each colour has a 'curve' that governs how intense or saturated it is. For example, the curve can be pushed to the top to fill the light image tones with flood colour.

see Screen Printing 223, Tonal Images 262

FINISHING TERM

Duplexing is the bonding of two materials, usually two different coloured stocks, to produce a single substrate. The use of duplexing creates a stronger, more robust material and also allows for different textures on either side.

Different materials can be duplexed such as plastic, shown above. In this example a red sheet and a white sheet have been duplexed and the top sheet has been etched away to reveal the one beneath.

☛ see Substrate 251

PRINTING TERM

Traditionally, a jacket around a hardback publication to offer protection against dirt and dust. Now it is more often an integral graphic extension of the book and a key device for promotion. Dust jackets are typically made from paper stock, although plastics can also be used. Experimenting with dust jacket design can produce exciting results, as this example shows.

Pictured is the dust jacket of *Pens Are My Friends*, a monographic compendium of the work of artist Jon Burgerman. It was created by Unthink, for publisher IdN. The fold-out dust jacket features one of Jon's images at large scale.

see Book 41

SCREEN TERM

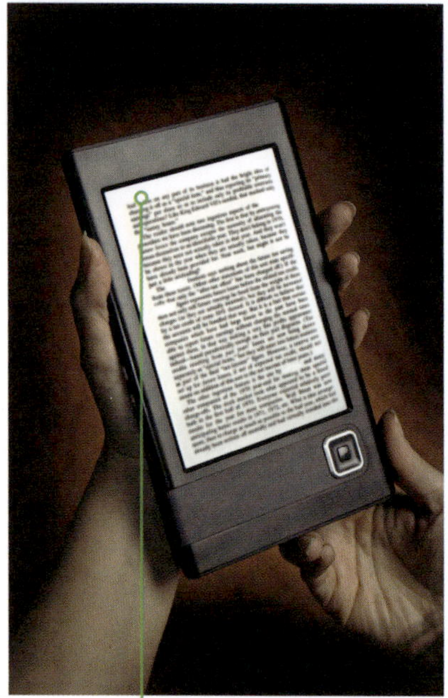

Electronic book
An e-book reader that uses a substrate printed with E Ink.

Electronic paper, manufactured by E Ink Corp, which uses a proprietary material that can be used for electronic displays such as e-book devices. An electronic display is formed by printing the ink on to a sheet of plastic film that is laminated to a layer of circuitry. The circuitry forms a pattern of pixels that are controlled by a display driver. These microcapsules are suspended in a liquid carrier medium allowing them to be printed, using existing screen printing processes, on to virtually any surface, including glass, plastic, fabric and paper.

E Embossing and Debossing

FINISHING TERM

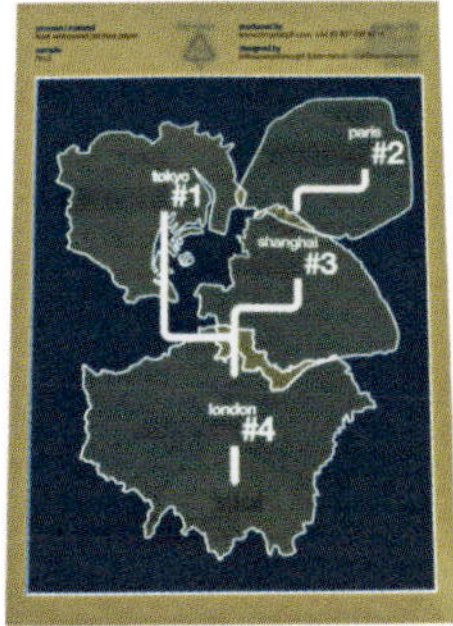

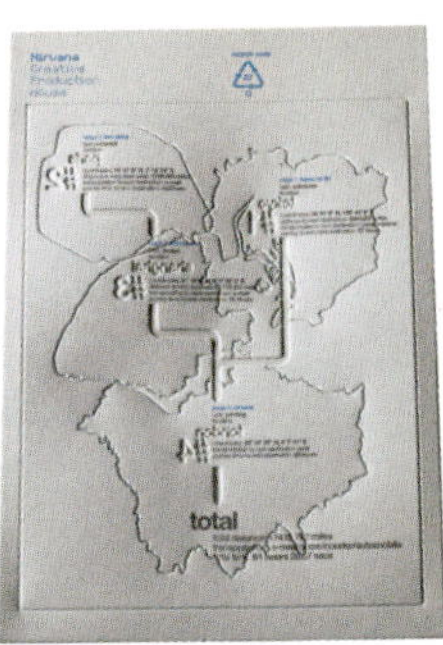

Pictured are a series of designs in different colourways by Research Studios; these designs feature a heat emboss.

Stamping a design into a substrate to produce a decorative raised or indented surface. For an emboss the stock is stamped underneath to leave an impression. A deboss is stamped from above. Copper and brass dies are more durable and so should be used for high print runs, for thick or abrasive stocks and for detailed designs.

The quality of an emboss or deboss depends on the quality of the design and the stock caliper. Thinner stocks can hold finer lines and more detail but there is a danger of puncturing the stock and intricate designs do not reproduce well. Thicker stocks are more robust but fine detail is lost; designs generally require thicker lines to reproduce well as the image has to press through more fibres. Soft papers are easier to emboss and coated stocks hold detail well but the coating may crack, so uncoated stock is better for deep embossing.

☛ see Blind Embossing and Debossing 39, Foil Block 104

FINISHING TERM

An additional fold made to a printed piece after the finishing processes – including folding – have been completed. An endorse fold is often added for distribution reasons; for example, an A4 newsletter may be endorse-folded to A5 to reduce the materials for mailing. In the example below, a US tabloid newsletter has been endorse-folded to letter size.

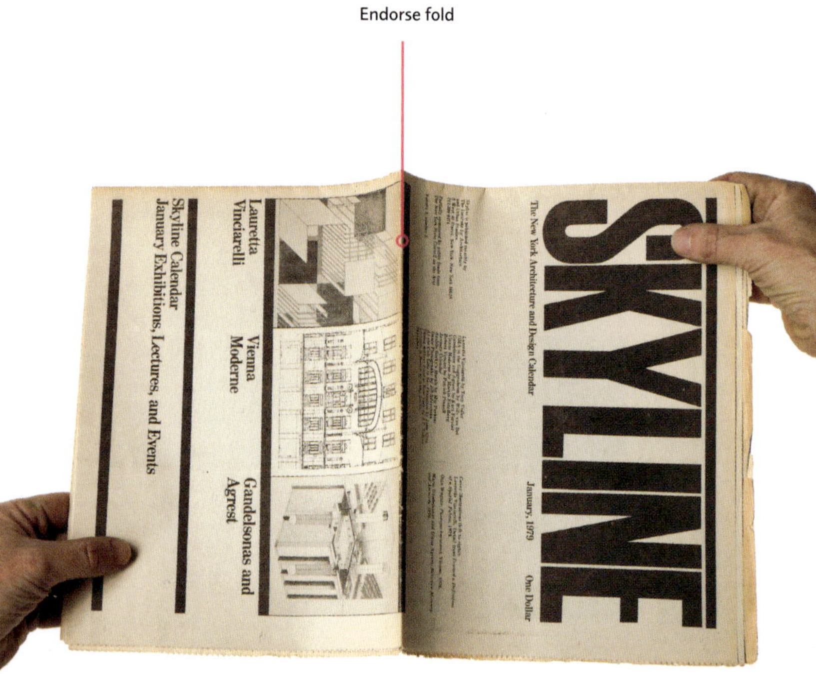

see Folding 106

E Endpapers

Also called endpages

PRINTING TERM

Heavy cartridge paper pages at the front and back of a hardback book, which are used to join the book block to the binding boards. Endpapers often depict maps or feature a decorative colour or design, such as the marbling designs seen here from various antique books.

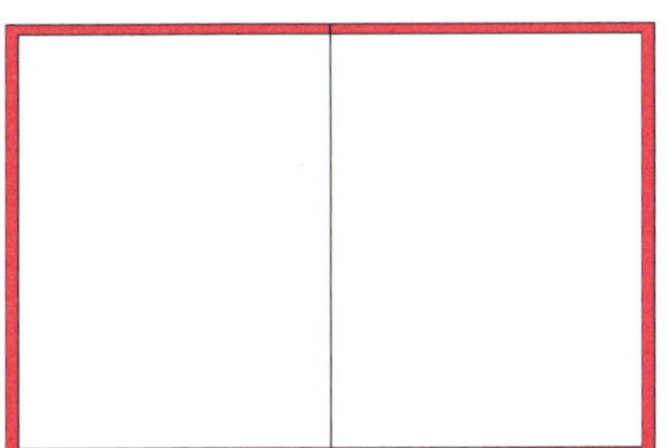

The endpaper choice is important as it essentially makes a frame that borders the pages when a book is laid flat. A designer needs to consider whether the colour and pattern will complement the content and design.

Antique
A book that is at least 100 years old and collectable or desirable because of its rarity, condition, utility or other unique features.

DESIGN TERM

An electronic file format used for storing graphics. EPS (Encapsulated PostScript) defines objects mathematically, which means they can be rescaled with smooth edges (no jaggies) and without loss of detail – an important consideration when text is present in a graphic. EPS is used to store vector graphics, which can be scaled to any size.

see Jaggies 146, Vector 275

Tools that facilitate the design process. Having the correct equipment available and using it properly helps a designer produce and present quality work in an efficient and cost-effective manner.

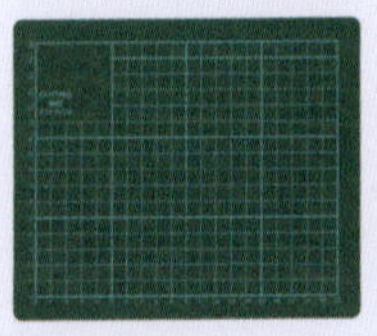

Cutting mat, roller, scalpels and sprays
A self-healing cutting mat, sharp scalpels, and a roller and correct sprays for making design dummies.

Loupe
For checking proofs, contact sheets and photographs.

Metal edge ruler
A straight, metal edge ruler is crucial for accurate cutting. For safety always 'cut-to-waste', meaning you cut away from yourself and into the area of the paper that is going to be thrown away.

Pantone books
A set of Pantone colour swatch books for checking and selecting colours.

Drawing tablet
A tool for sketching design ideas and/or retouching images. The action of the tablet allows fine hand detail to be applied to electronic files, freeing the designer from the actions of a traditional mouse and keyboard.

Memory sticks
Useful for transporting images and files. It is also necessary to keep back-ups of files and images handy in case anything gets corrupted at print stage.

DESIGN TERM

Recycled paper: paper made up of consumer waste / recycled fibre.

Vegetable inks: ink produced with biodegradable vegetable oil, rather than petroleum solvents, as the vehicle for carrying pigment.

Precise print runs: printing no more copies than are needed.

Chlorine-free paper: paper produced with no chlorine chemistry, which can pollute rivers.

Totally chlorine-free (TCF): papers made from virgin fibre that has not been bleached with chlorine or chlorine-based compounds

Processed chlorine-free (PCF): papers that contain up to 100% recycled content that has not been re-bleached with chlorine compounds.

Elemental chlorine-free (ECF): virgin paper processed without elemental chlorine but with chlorine derivatives such as chlorine dioxide.

Carbon offset: a financial instrument representing a reduction in greenhouse gas emissions, measured in metric tonnes of carbon dioxide-equivalent (CO2e). Carbon offsetting is used to fund projects that prevent the emission of a tonne of greenhouse gases for every tonne caused.

Sustainable Forestry Initiative (SFI): a North American label indicating that wood and paper products are from well-managed forests, backed by a rigorous, third-party certification audit.

Forest Stewardship Council (FSC): certified forest products made using environmentally responsible, socially beneficial and economically viable management of forests. Forest Management Certificates are issued to enterprises that meet FSC-approved standards of forest management. Chain-of-Custody Certificates are issued to processing and trade companies that handle, label and advertise certified products.

A set of moral principles. A design seeks to convince an audience of a certain viewpoint and the designer is central to establishing how that message is put across. At a wider level, ethical design encompasses the use of eco-friendly products and processes to offset the damage caused by traditional print processes.

DESIGN TERM

Companion fonts that carry additional and specific characters. Not all fonts have an accompanying expert set, so you should plan whether you'll need these special marks.

Standard font

ABCDEFGHIJKLMNOPQRSTUVWXYZ
abcdefghijklmnopqrstuvwxyz 1234567890

A standard character set contains majuscules, minuscules and numbers.

Expert set

¼ ½ ¾ ⅛ ⅜ ⅝ ⅞ ⅓ ⅔

Expert sets contain proper fractions.

ff fi fl ffi ffl

Expert sets contain common ligatures, which are characters formed for specific letter combinations that are prone to interfere when set together.

ABCDEFGHIJKLMNOPQRSTUVWXYZ

Small caps have line weights that are proportionally correct, which means that they can be used within body copy without looking out of place.

1234567890

Old-style numerals have descenders that drop below the baseline and only the 6 and 8 have the same proportions as their lining numeral counterparts.

ABCDEFGHJKMNPQR

Swash characters have extended or exaggerated decorative calligraphic swashes, usually on the capitals.

SCREEN TERM

The manner in which digital information is encoded for storage by a computer. These can be broken into three main categories: **saved files**, **sending files** and **capture files**.

SAVED FILES

TIFF: a continuous tone file format for lossless compression of images that are to be printed.

EPS: a file format for scalable graphic elements.

JPEG: a continuous tone file format for lossy compression of images that are to be used for the web.

GIF: a file format for compressing line art and flat colour images, which are to be used for web applications.

PICT: A Mac-based format for compressing images with predominantly plain background colours.

BMP: A format for uncompressed 24- or 32-bit colour images used for graphic manipulation.

SENDING FILES

PDF: a portable document format used for sending files between the designer, client and printer. A PDF embeds all the necessary font and graphic files for the design.

CAPTURE FILES

RAW: the format for capturing maximum continuous tone colour information when taking photographs; a file that is not compressed or processed. RAW files need to be converted in order to use the images.

see GIF 115, JPEG 148, RAW 209, TIFF 259

PRINTING TERM

Aa Aa

Aa Aa

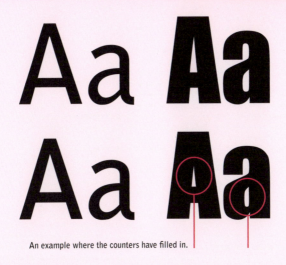

An example where the counters have filled in.

A printing error that occurs when dot gain reduces the counters of letters, making them more difficult to read. Fill in is more likely to occur when rougher, more absorbent stocks are used and where a typeface has smaller counters. Bell (above, left column) is cut with large counters, which will remain open when they are printed at small sizes. The apex point of the counter on the capital A is deeper than on most other typefaces, creating an ink well that allows for fill in during printing without compromising legibility. Impact (above, right column) was designed as a display type and so it has smaller counters, which are subject to fill in when printed small or where there is dot gain.

see Dot Gain / Dot Size 78, Font / Typeface 108, Type Anatomy 298

DESIGN TERM

Photographic devices that are used to change the presentation of a final image. A filter can make an adjustment that is so subtle the viewer barely recognises the enhancement. Filters are also available as part of image manipulation and photo-editing programs and they can be used to create some interesting and startling graphic effects, as shown below.

Sepia

Gradient map

Median

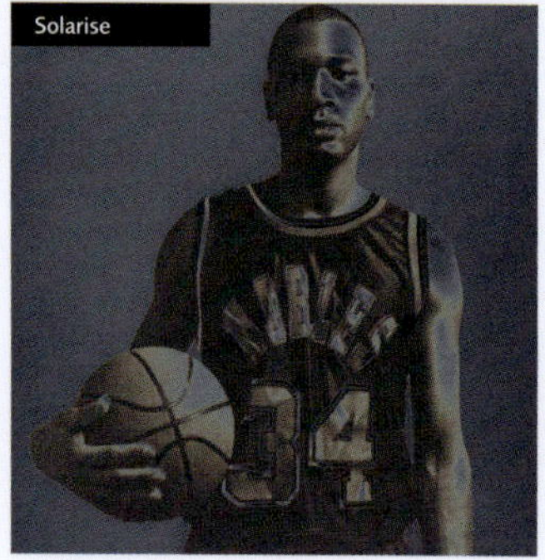
Solarise

see Image Manipulation 138

FINISHING TERM

A wide range of processes that provide the finishing touches to a job once the substrate has been printed. Finishing processes include die cutting, binding, special print techniques, laminating, folding, foil blocking, varnishing and screen printing, all of which can transform an ordinary-looking piece into something much more interesting and dynamic. Finishing processes can add decorative elements to a printed piece, such as the shimmer of a foil block or the texture of an emboss. Finishing techniques also add functionality to a design and can even be a constituent part of a publications format; for example, a matte laminate to protect a substrate, making it last longer. Although the application of print finishing techniques signals the end of the production process, these techniques should not be considered as afterthoughts but as an integral part of a design that needs to be considered at the planning stage.

Pictured is an example of screen printing, a process used for substrates such as plastics, which cannot be printed by a traditional press. This prints in white, a colour that cannot be produced by the traditional four-colour printing process.

see Die Cutting 73, Embossing and Debossing 87, Substrate 251

SCREEN TERM

Adobe software program used for creating digital animations and interactivity on webpages and other digital media. Flash allows a user to develop and manipulate vector and raster graphics to create animations that can be viewed with Adobe Flash Player, a freeware viewer. Flash enables websites to have smooth animation transitions and seamless links from page to page. However, it does not allow for search engine optimisation (SEO) and it lacks compliance capability; for example, users who are visually impaired would be unable to make text larger or change its colour so it is more readable, and the spoken word system will not function.

Pictured is a website created by Gavin Ambrose for Urbik, which uses Flash to provide a seamless viewing environment. Instead of having a series of pages connected by a menu, this site has a series of frames that are reproduced in one continuous strip, minimising 'clicking' and making use of scrolling.

see Menu 168, Scrolling 224

A method of visually organising the order of a publication. A flatplan allows a designer to determine how the editorial and advertising content of a publication fits in the space available and to establish a certain pace in a publication. Colour coding may be used to identify different types of content, as shown below.

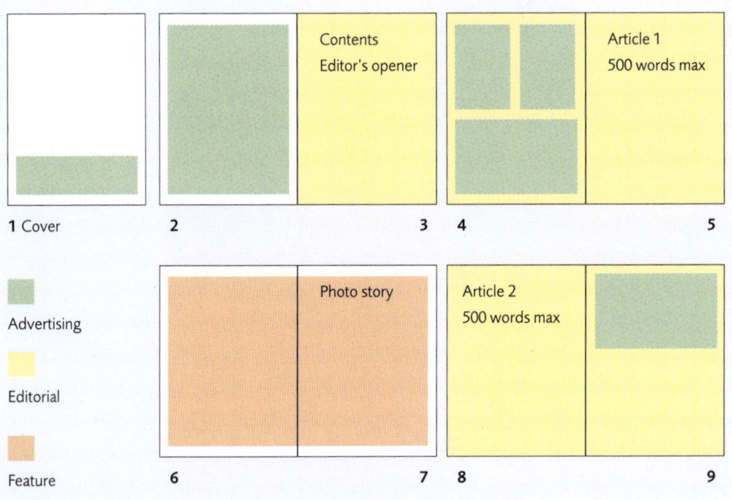

see Thumbnail 258

FINISHING TERM

A covering made by fixing woollen refuse or vegetable fibre dust to paper or board. Flock has a velvety or nap-like finish; it adds a tactile element to a design and is as much about 'feel' as look. It is not generally used for printing, although it is possible; it is more often used with foil blocking, as shown in the example below, by Thomas Manss & Company.

see Foil Block 104

PRINTING TERM

An image that has been flipped and printed in reverse. A flop is a printing error that may occur when images are supplied as transparencies. This happens less frequently now that images are supplied digitally, but transparencies are still used for high-end jobs such as art books and advertising. Designers sometimes also flop an image for compositional purposes, but beware of doing this if there is any text in the image, such as on clothing or products.

see Transparencies 264

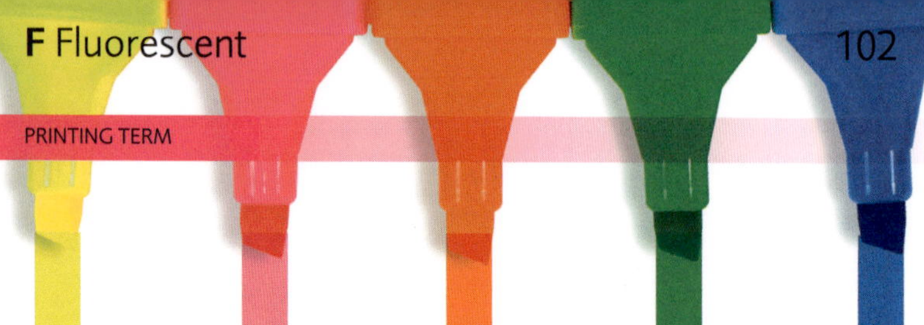

PRINTING TERM

A colour so brilliant that it apparently gives off light. The use of fluorescent inks will produce bright colours on a design, particularly on coloured stocks. Fluorescent inks may even be added to the CMYK process colours to intensify them. On press fluorescent inks do not behave like regular colours; higher quantities are usually needed to achieve the intensity required, and they are harder to match to the colours in swatch books. (Please note this page has not been printed with fluorescent colours.)

The Pantone colour system provides the following fluorescent colours that print as special colours:

Colour	Pantone Uncoated	Pantone Coated
Blue	801U	801C
Green	802U	802C
Yellow	803U	803C
Orange	804U	804C
Red	805U	805C
Raspberry	806U	806C
Purple	807U	807C

These can also be mixed to make a secondary set of colours; for instance, mixing 2 parts Pantone 802 with 14 parts Pantone 803 creates a bright lime colour.

Pantone	Mix
808 C/U	8 parts Pantone 801 with 8 parts Pantone 802
809 C/U	2 parts Pantone 802 with 14 parts Pantone 803
810 C/U	12.5 parts Pantone 803 with 4 parts Pantone 804
811 C/U	8 parts Pantone 804 with 8 parts Pantone 805
812 C/U	6 parts Pantone 805 with 10 parts Pantone 806
813 C/U	7 parts Pantone 806 with 9 parts Pantone 807
814 C/U	13 parts Pantone 807 with 3 parts Pantone 801

Also called fly sheets PRINTING TERM

A thin paper stock within a book. Fly sheets are often used to protect colour plates. They are not to be confused with endpapers, which are used to join the book block to a cover.

see Book 41, Endpapers 89, Stock 246

FINISHING TERM *Also called foil stamp, heat stamp or foil emboss*

A print finishing process whereby a coloured foil is pressed on to a substrate using a heated die. Foil blocking can be used to add an attractive shiny finish to specific design elements such as title text.

Pictured is a flyer, created by Unthink to promote a new custom design service in Habitat's Dublin store, which features a green foil block in a gold mirror board substrate.

Notice how the foil block die leaves a slight deboss in the substrate surface, which adds a tactile element.

see Embossing and Debossing 87, Finishing 97, Substrate 251

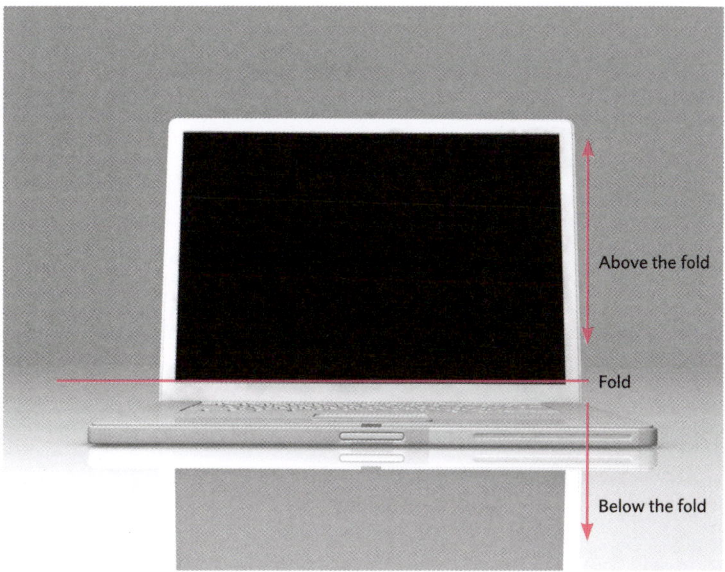

The point on a webpage that delimits the visible and non-visible content. Web technology allows for the creation of endless pages but there are screen limits, which means that users have to scroll down to view all the pages. A screen fold is a relative, movable position determined by the size of the screen and its resolution, with the bottom of the screen being the fold. Web advertisers refer to the top half of a webpage, which is initially visible when the page loads, as being above the fold.

☛ see Resolution 213, Scrolling 224

FINISHING TERM

The way in which a printed sheet is turned into a more compact form or signature. Different folding methods produce different structures but all make use of the basic valley and mountain folds: alternate folds made in opposing directions to create a series of peaks and troughs. Each folding method will require a different imposition plan to organise the pages for printing.

Held horizontally, a valley fold has a central crease at the bottom with the panels rising upwards to form the valley sides; a mountain fold has a central crease at the top, like a mountain ridge, with the panels falling downwards.

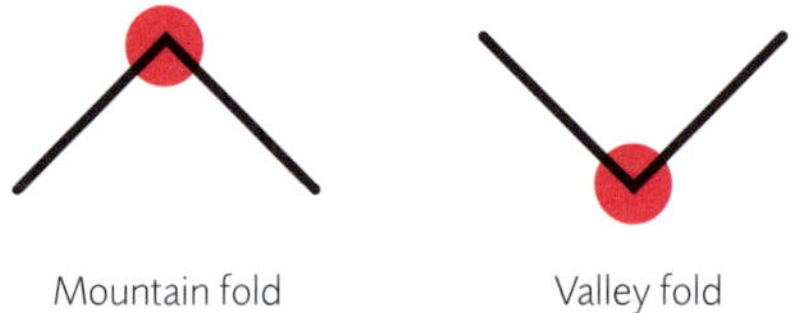

Mountain fold

Valley fold

☛ see Imposition 139, Signatures 234

DESIGN TERM

A page number. Folios are traditionally placed on the outer edge of the bottom margin where they are easy to find to aid navigation when thumbing through a book. However, they can be centred (as above) or located near the inside margin, at the top or foot of the page; they may even be centred in the outside margin. Having folios centred under the text block adds harmony; positioning them to the outer margin adds dynamism to a layout as they are more noticeable and act as visual weights.

The term folio is also used to refer to a large format book, where the inner sheets are only folded once before binding. It can also mean a page or leaf of a book.

see Leaves and Printed Pages 157

DESIGN TERM

A font is the physical means used to create a typeface, whether it be a typewriter, a stencil, letterpress blocks or a piece of PostScript code. In common usage, font and typeface are used synonymously. A typeface is a collection of characters that have the same distinct design. While one can ask 'What typeface is that?' or 'What font was used in that publication?', it would be inaccurate to ask, 'What font is that?' when looking at a design.

Pictured here are the strikers of a typewriter: these are the font. The specific pattern of the shapes they carry are the typeface.

PRINTING TERM

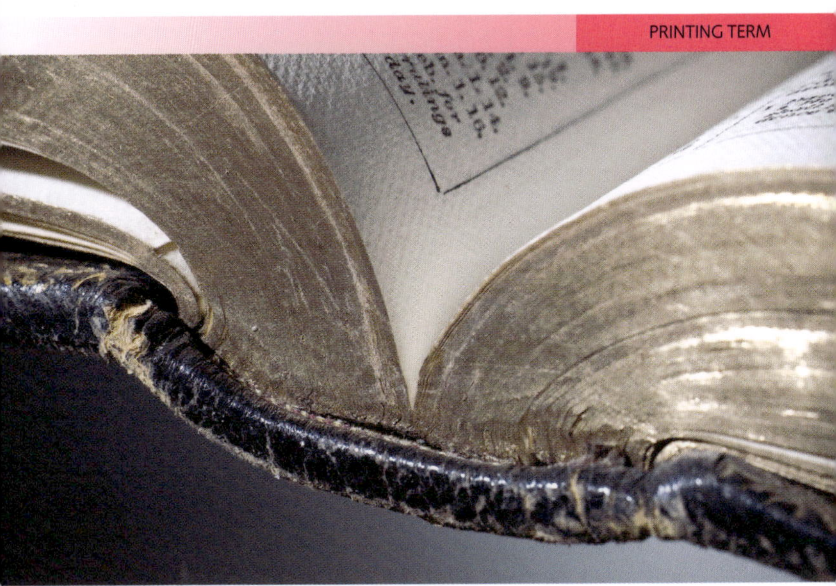

The printing or application of gold leaf on the cut edges of a book. Originally used to add protection and longevity to Bibles (shown above) and ledgers, fore-edge printing is now more often used for decorative effect.

Fore-edge printing creates an impression of worth and value; it implies that the book should be kept and treasured.

☞ see Book 41, French Fold 112

F Four-colour Black

DESIGN TERM

K: 100

C:100 M:100 Y:100 K: 100

The darkest black that can be printed; it is produced when all four process colours are overprinted on each other. The greyscale image (top) prints with the process black. Notice how a beefier, blacker result can be achieved by printing with all four process colours (bottom).

see Overprinting 182, Shiners and Bouncers 232

DESIGN TERM

Part or portion of a whole number. Fractions can be represented in two ways in typography; more specifically, it is the presentation of the bar that separates the numerator and denominator. Fractions with a horizontal bar are nut or en fractions while those with a diagonal bar are em fractions. Em fractions, which are more pleasing to the eye and are commonly included with expert type sets, are so-called because the bar is an em in length. A solidus (forward slash) cannot be used as its angle, length and position on the baseline is wrong for expressing fractions. Most fonts include a fraction bar, which is a kerned character that allows a designer to construct fractions and, unlike a solidus, it will not push the numerals away a full em space. When building fractions, the character weight is lighter and so it may be necessary to use a medium weight to match the regular font. Nut or en fractions are less common and have a bar that is an en in length. En fractions are increasingly called nut fractions to avoid confusion with the em fraction.

$^{1}/_{2}$ 1/2 ½ $\frac{1}{2}$

This fraction is set using subscript and superscript characters and a solidus. It appears untidy and disjointed; note how the angle of bar is wrong.

This fraction uses baseline shift to bring the 2 character to a more acceptable position, improving the overall homogeneity.

This fraction is a proper fraction created by a fraction font. Note how compact it is, helped by the angle of the fraction bar.

This is a nut fraction. See how much smaller and tighter this arrangement is.

F French Fold

FINISHING TERM

A printing and binding technique, used in a number of different ways:

A to form booklet printing on one side only, common with invitations;

B to form an eight-page section that will be bound and trimmed;

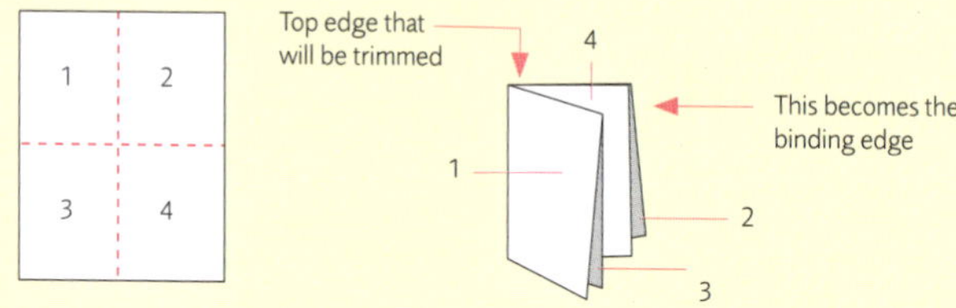

and C a method of binding where single sheets are folded back on themselves to form a cavity, as shown below.

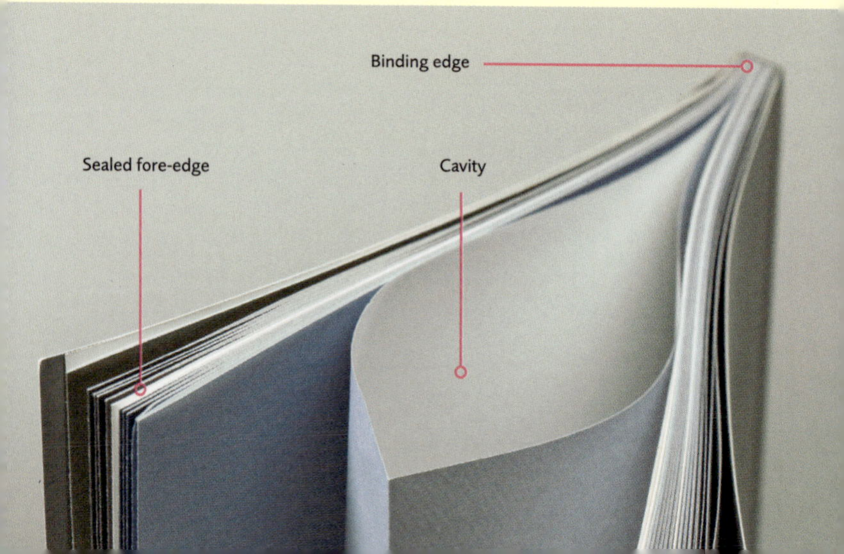

Binding edge

Sealed fore-edge

Cavity

FINISHING TERM

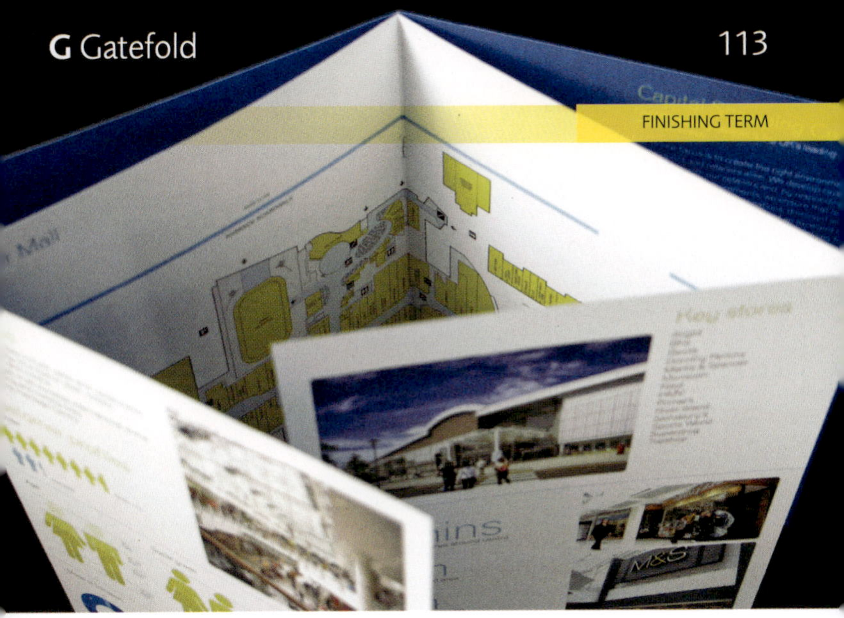

Pictured is a brochure created by To The Point, which features a gatefold.

A useful means of allocating space within a brochure for more panoramic material. On a gatefold both sides fold out, as opposed to a throwout, where only one folds out. When designing a gatefold, you need to make the fold-out pages shorter than the book size, so they can fold into the binding edge, as shown below.

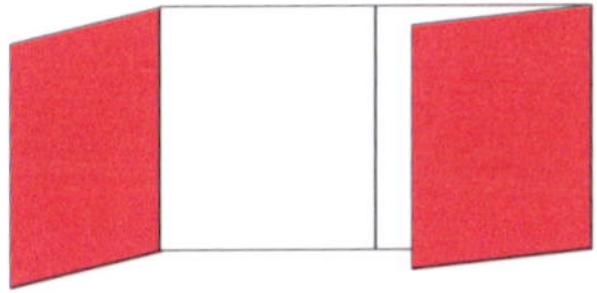

see Throwout / Throw Up 257

PRINTING TERM

THE APPEARANCE OF A FAINT PRINTED IMAGE ON A PRINTED SHEET. IT IS DIFFICULT TO FORESEE WHERE GHOSTING MAY OCCUR AND IT CAN DEVELOP IMMEDIATELY AFTER PRINTING OR WHILE DRYING. GHOSTING CAN BE CORRECTED BY CHANGING THE COLOUR PRINTING SEQUENCE, THE INKS OR THE PAPER; CHANGING TO A PRESS WITH A DRIER; PRINTING THE PROBLEM AREA IN A SEPARATE PASS THROUGH THE PRESS; OR REDUCING THE NUMBER OF SHEETS ON THE DRYING RACKS.

see Printing 200

SCREEN TERM

An image file format used for storing images with up to 256 colours. A GIF (Graphics Interchange Format) uses lossless LZW compression. GIFs are widely used for web graphics because of their small file size.

GIFs obtain a small file size by excluding as many colour shades as possible while maintaining reasonable image representation. GIFs work best for flat coloured graphics, such as logos, rather than continuous tone images such as photographs.

Animated GIF

A file that uses several GIF images to create a rudimentary animation. Animated GIFs are used for logos and flat colour images such as emoticons.

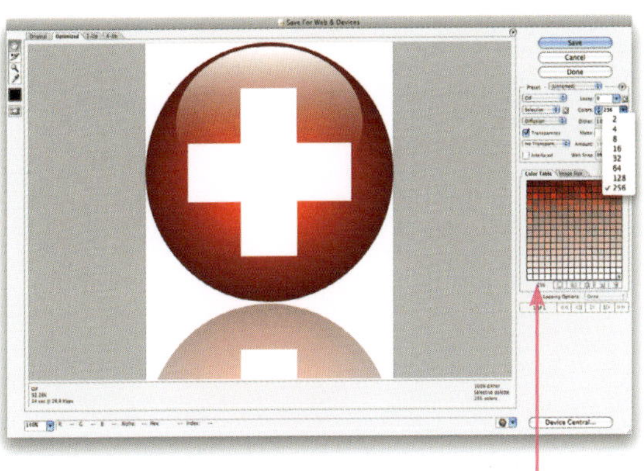

When saving a GIF file you have the option of reducing the number of colours it contains. As standard, 256 are used but this online logo, for instance, could be successfully reproduced using as few as 36 colours.

Reducing the number of colours means you can reduce the file size.

see Compression 60, Continuous Tone 65

DESIGN TERM

The use of one or more colours to create an increasing or decreasing tone effect. In a two-colour gradient, one colour typically gets stronger or darker as the other gets weaker or lighter, such as the background behind the desk shown here. However, the use of gradients is prone to the appearance of a banding pattern, which is introduced by the halftone screens simulating the subtle tone changes across the image. Banding can be avoided by adding noise into the gradient to disperse or dither the colour, which creates a more random pattern to the screen angles. Shown above is a design by Gavin Ambrose for Fleming & Howland. Photographer Xavier Young shot the furniture against a gradient background, creating a feeling of luxury.

see Banding 28

DESIGN TERM

A photo-editing tool that matches the brightness values in a digital image with the colours in the gradient specified. Gradient maps can be used to make dramatic colour interventions, such as those shown here. The range of effects varies depending on the gradient used.

see Brightness 44, Filters 96, Gradient 116

DESIGN TERM

The grain in photographic film is created by light-sensitive silver halide crystals. The crystals have different sizes depending on the film speed. Faster films, which are more reactive to light, are made from larger silver halide crystals and produce grainier images.

Digital image software uses noise to add the effect of grain to an image.

Noise
Random application of pixels to an image to create the effect of photographs shot on high-speed film.

G Grain (Paper)

PRINTING TERM

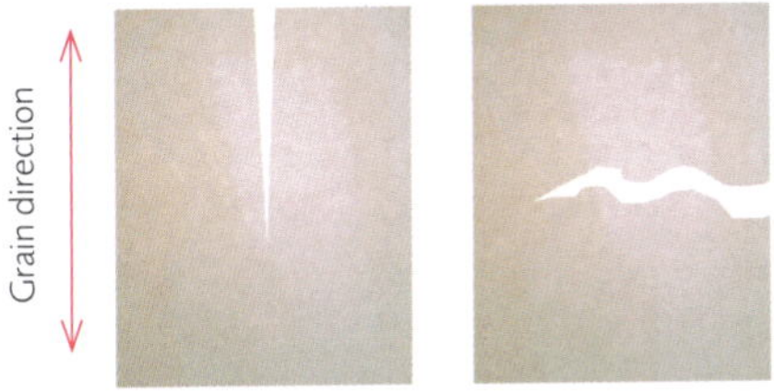

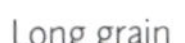

Long grain Short grain

Paper grain is a characteristic of the direction in which the paper leaves the paper-making machine. If a book is printed with the paper grain parallel to the spine it will open more easily and lie flat. Grain direction can be determined by tearing the paper, as shown above. The tear will be straight when parallel to the grain (left), and it will be jagged across the grain (right).

DESIGN TERM

NONSENSICAL TEXT USED AS A PLACEHOLDER IN A DESIGN BEFORE REAL COPY IS INSERTED.

IT IS WORTH NOTING THAT GREEKING ISN'T NECESSARILY GREEK; THE NAME IS A REFERENCE TO THE PHRASE 'ALL GREEK TO ME', WHICH MEANS SOMETHING IS IMPOSSIBLE TO UNDERSTAND, MUCH LIKE A FOREIGN LANGUAGE.

GREEKING TEXT CAN BE LATIN, JUMBLED ENGLISH, ESPERANTO, JABBERWOCKY (A REFERENCE TO NONSENSE VERSE WRITTEN BY LEWIS CARROLL) OR EVEN KLINGON (FROM THE *STAR TREK* SERIES). CARE SHOULD BE TAKEN THOUGH, AS SOME OF THESE CAN BE DISTRACTING AND THE POINT OF GREEKING IS THAT IT SHOULDN'T BE READ.

DESIGN TERM

An image that contains shades of grey, black and white. A digital greyscale image is one where the value of pixels contain only a single sample or colour set. This means greyscale images contain a myriad of greys, in between full black and absolute white. In contrast, a bitmap or binary image contains only black or white, with no grey values in between.

Pictured are greyscale images used in a catalogue by Faydherbe / de Vringer.

see Brightness 44, Pixel / Pixelation 195

PRINTING TERM *Also known as grammage or paper density*

The common metric measurement for paper weight. GSM, or grams per square metre, is a measurement based on the weight of the standard ISO A0 paper size, which has an area of 1 square metre. The relationship represented by the ISO paper size system means that it is simple to calculate the weight of a printed piece. For example, a standard A4 80 GSM sheet paper weighs 5 grams (one sixteenth of an A0 page). In the USA paper is measured by its basis weight, which is a measure of the mass (in pounds) of an uncut ream of 500 sheets of a given basis size. It should be noted that an increase in paper weight typically means thicker paper and greater opacity.

see Bulk 45, Paper 187

Also called cutter

FINISHING TERM

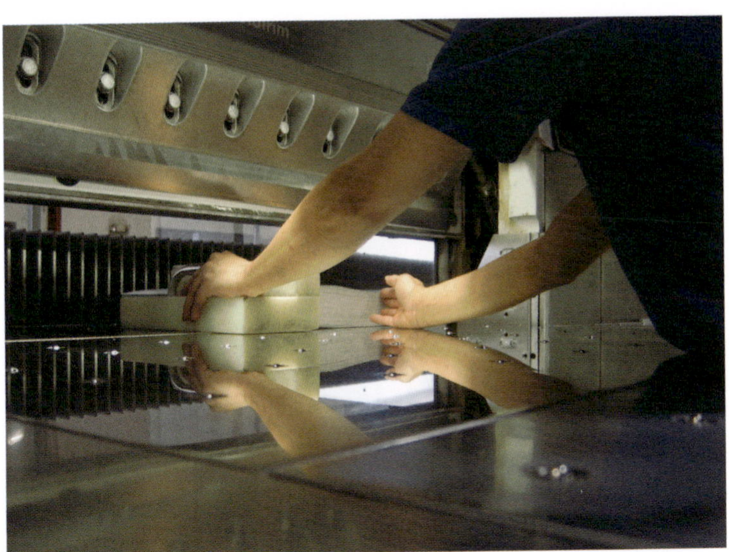

A machine that cuts a stack of printed paper stock to the required size with a heavy-duty blade. Guillotines can be used to cut hundreds of sheets of paper at a time, depending on the stock and its bulk, although lower cutting quantities results in a more accurate cut. They can be operated manually, electrically or hydraulically, and may be programmed to make a series of automatic cuts.

Cutter draw

Where too many sheets are cut at one time, the guillotine has a tendency to draw across the paper block making a poor cut, rather than cutting in the exact same place on each sheet. This can be prevented by requesting that a job be cut in small batches.

☛ see Paper 187, Stock 246

PRINTING TERM

The space that comprises the central alleyway between two pages at the spine. Gutter is also used to refer to the space between text columns, which provides a visual break. In many designs, gutters are often page areas of dead space. Pictured is a spread created by Webb & Webb, which features a photo printed over the gutter at the spine. The accurate alignment or registration of the two halves of the image can be affected by the image's position in the publication and the number of pages it has to be folded around. The closer the image to the centre of the folded signature, the more accurate the alignment.

☛ see Column 58, Registration 211, Signatures 234, Spine 240

Also called half leather FINISHING TERM

A book binding method that uses a leather binding on the spine, and perhaps the corners, with paper, cloth or other material used to cover the sides.

The pink triangles show where protective corners would be placed.

see Binding 34

DESIGN TERM

The series of dots produced during the screening process to prepare a continuous tone image, such as a photograph, for printing. The four-colour printing process creates halftone separations for each of the CMYK process colours. During printing, the different colour halftone dots combine to produce continuous tone colour images. Halftone 'dots' can be lines, dots, ellipses or squares and a designer can control and change their screen angles, frequencies and size. Different sizes create tonal variation.

Pictured is a poster created by Faydherbe / de Vringer that features the use of halftone images.

see CMYK 54, Continuous Tone 65

The process of binding a book by hand. Hand binding is typically a means of fitting a casebinding on a book using similar materials as used by professional binders. The illustrations below show the case into which the book block will be bound, with endpapers. The block will be glued into the hollow.

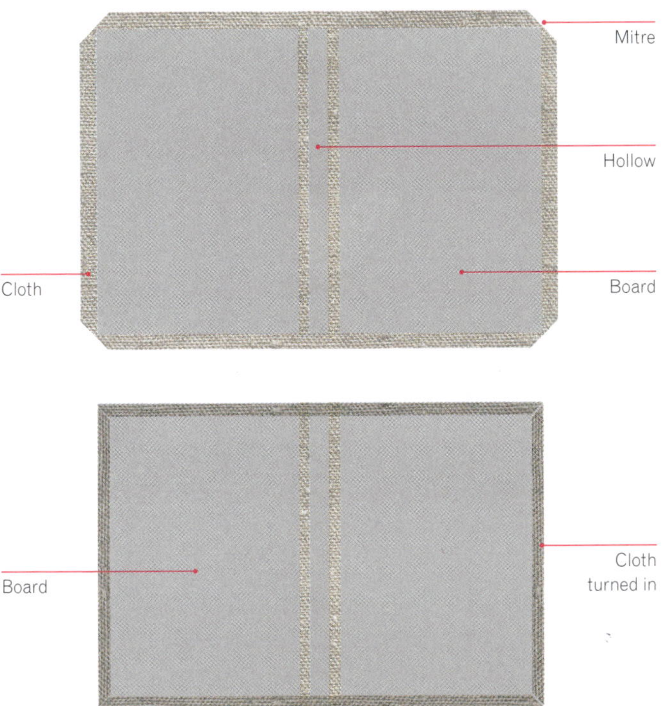

A paper substrate made by a dilute suspension of fibres in water. The suspension is drained through a screen to form a mat of randomly interwoven fibres and then pressed to remove the water, contributing to the paper's typical 'handmade' visual characteristics. Handmade paper does not typically have a specific grain as the alignment of the fibres is not controlled by the production process. The use of different sources of paper fibre and colourants imparts different colours to the stock. Once dry the paper may have further finishing, such as rolling to produce a smoother surface; this also affects its qualities and characteristics. Handmade paper produced in a wooden frame or deckle has irregular, wavy edges called deckle edges.

Deckle edge

The uneven edge that results from the papermaking process. This can be trimmed or left for decorative purposes

FINISHING TERM

A piece of cloth tape that covers the top or bottom of the spine and offers both protection and a decorative quality. Headband tape is available in a range of different colours and colour combinations, including stripes. It may be used to add a distinct touch to a publication, such as the yellow-and-green band in the book shown here.

see Book 41, Spine 240

PRINTING TERM

A range of six process colours used for printing. The hexachrome printing system is an improvement on the four-colour printing process and works in the same way, but with the addition of green and orange to improve the gamut of colours. A gamut is every colour combination that it is possible to produce with a given set of colourants on a particular device or system. Colour printing systems cannot reproduce the full spectral colour gamut that the human eye can see, but hexachrome can produce 90% of the Pantone PMS colours. The CMYK gamut produces fewer than 70%.

Hexachrome printing colours

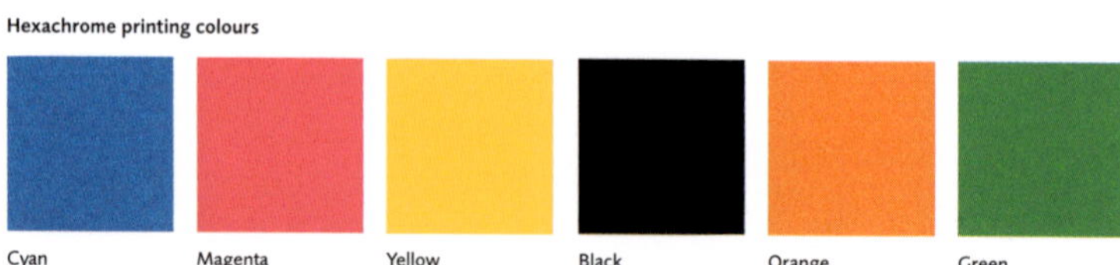

see CMYK 54

Hickey

Also called bullseye

PRINTING TERM

A spot of ink deposited on a sheet. This printing error is caused by a particle of grit on the printing plate.

A similar printing defect on laser printers is a halo: a white edge that surrounds a toned area. It occurs when fringe fields, caused by surface potential differences, are generated at the edge of a toned area; these pull charged toner particles away from the edges of the area to receive toner.

The presence of hickey printing errors are circled in the two print jobs above. On the left, the presence of dust on the printing bed has caused a halo-shaped hickey. On the right, a printing plate needs clearing of hair and other debris, which has appeared on the printed sheet.

☛ see Loupe 165

FINISHING TERM

A pattern produced on a photosensitive medium, which has been exposed by holography and then photographically developed. Holography records the light scattered from an object so that the recorded image changes as the viewing position changes, making the hologram appear three-dimensional. Holograms are used for security tags on bank notes and credit cards as the replication process requires relatively expensive and specialised equipment.

Pictured is a range of Canadian banknotes, which feature a hologram strip that bears the value of the bill.

see Diffraction Foil 74

The predominant markup language for web pages. HTML (Hyper Text Markup Language) is universal and supported by most web browsers. HTML provides a means to define the structure and presentation of a webpage, such as the position, colour and size of different elements. The visual presentation possible with HTML may be less dynamic compared with technologies such as Flash, but it has the advantage that keywords included in the HTML coding can be picked up by search engines.

SEO

SEO (search engine optimisation) improves the volume and quality of traffic to a website from search engines.

Keywords

Words that help retrieve web content using a search engine.

Tag

A keyword or phrase assigned to web page, PDF or other resource to help describe it and aid searches.

Analytics

The use of software to analyse the performance of a website or e-marketing campaign.

PHP

A general-purpose scripting language used to create dynamic content that interacts with databases.

DESIGN TERM

The colour reflected or transmitted from an object. Hue refers to the unique characteristic of a colour that helps us visually distinguish one colour from another. A hue is formed by different wavelengths of visible light and expressed as a value between 0 and 360 on the colour wheel. Changing hue values will dramatically alter the colour of an image.

The hue of the original image (left) has been altered (above). Hue functions like a wheel: one extreme runs into another, with myriad colours in between. In this instance, the green hues of a leaf have been altered to red. Hue is normally used in conjunction with saturation and lightness to create a balanced effect.

H Hyperlink / Hypertext

Also called link

SCREEN TERM

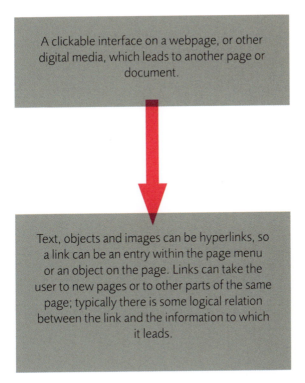

A clickable interface on a webpage, or other digital media, which leads to another page or document.

Text, objects and images can be hyperlinks, so a link can be an entry within the page menu or an object on the page. Links can take the user to new pages or to other parts of the same page; typically there is some logical relation between the link and the information to which it leads.

see Menu 168

DESIGN TERM

The use of a hyphen to divide a word at the end of a text line. When using justified text, hyphenation is often necessary to produce a visually attractive text block. Hyphenation is controllable both in terms of where words are broken and the number of successive lines that can be hyphenated. Typographically, more than two successive lines of text that end in hyphens is undesirable.

A hypho is a hyphenated widow that leaves half a word on a line, as shown at the end of the previous paragraph. Hyphos can be removed by reducing letter or word spacing, or by rewriting.

Without hyphenation, a text block will become increasingly loose and baggy due to excess word spacing. This is unsightly and produces an uneven looking result for the text block.

see Orphans and Widows 180, Variable Space 273

A system of codes used to indicate changes to the reproduction of photographs and other images. Image correction marks are annotated during proofing, in a process known as marking up, to communicate corrections and the specific areas to which they should be applied. These include:

Instructions	**Margin mark**
Passed for press	✓
Reproof	△ Note: reproof number
Reduce contrast	□
Increase contrast	■
Improve detail	□■
Make softer	U
Make sharper	Λ
Uneven tint	◐
Repair broken type, tint or rule	X
Improve register	⧉
Correct slur	

Process colour	**Increase**	**Decrease**
Yellow	Y+	Y-
Magenta	M+	M-
Cyan	C+	C-
Black	B+ (or K+)	B- (or K-)

PRINTING TERM

A variety of processes that can be used to change the appearance of an image. Image manipulation ranges from removing blemishes to changing backgrounds, colours, colour correction and the addition of elements. Pictured is an illustration created by Katie Fechtmann, which features a digitally manipulated image.

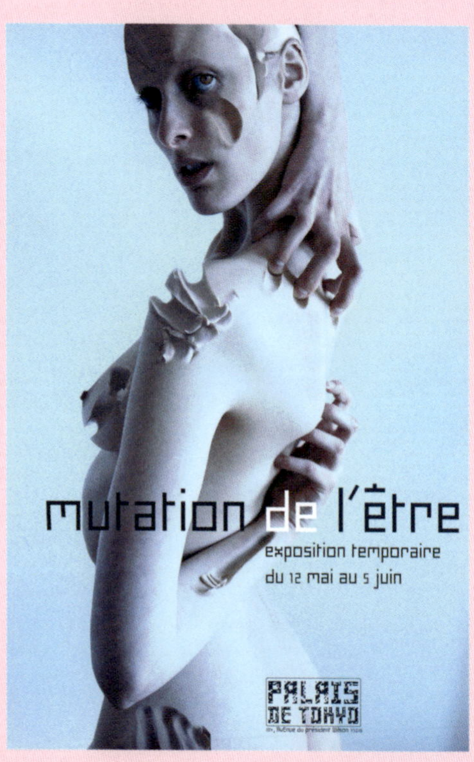

I Imposition

PRINTING TERM

A plan that shows the arrangement of the different pages of a publication. The imposition contains information needed by the printer to produce the job, such as identifying the stock to be used for the different sections, the printing colours, and how and where any spot colours are to be used. An imposition plan helps a designer to plan the colour fall so that all the pages that need printing with a certain colour can be grouped together to improve efficiency and reduce costs. The imposition plan can look confusing: some pages appear upside down, because the pages of a section print on a sheet that is folded and trimmed. Providing you know how a publication is to be printed, a simple way to imagine its sections is as horizontal strips of pages, such as the imposition plan for this book, which is formed from 16-page sections. Pages to view refers to the number of pages that will be printed on one side of a sheet of stock.

Signature one

1	2	3	4	5	6	7	8	9	10	11	12	13	14	15	16

Signature two

17	18	19	20	21	22	23	24	25	26	27	28	29	30	31	32

Signature three

33	34	35	36	37	38	39	40	41	42	43	44	45	46	47	48

Signature four

49	50	51	52	53	54	55	56	57	58	59	60	61	62	63	64

The example above is a typical impostion plan. In this arrangement, alternate spreads print CMYK, for photographic images, while the reverse pages print black only; these carry text. An alternative would be to bunch all the colour in signatures one and four. In this instance signatures one and four would be printed together and then cut. A printer is usually able to advise what is possible and to help arrange the printing and pages to suit the job.

see Colour Fall 57, Signatures 234

I Impression

PRINTING TERM

The print run of a publication, printed at one time from the same set of type. In book-making, each impression or print run is known as an edition, with each edition numbered sequentially.

Impression can also mean a single copy of a printing; or a mark or image produced on the surface of a substrate by pressure, as shown in this example by Studio Myerscough.

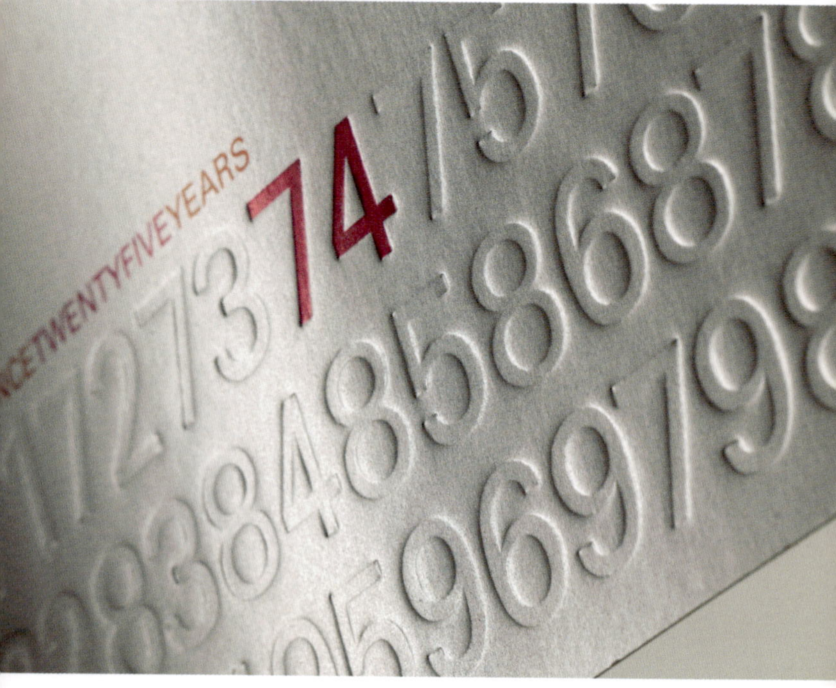

see Printing 200, Substrate 251

PRINTING TERM

A pigmented liquid, paste or powder, which is used for printing, drawing or writing. The most common printing ink is black, followed by the other three process colours used in the four-colour printing process. However, there is also a wide range of special colour inks available, which are identified through the numbers of the Pantone Matching System. Specialist inks can be used to reproduce a wide range of visual effects or impact specific performance characteristics, such as the following:

Wax-free ink
Wax-free ink is used for high-heat printing jobs, such as laser printing. Wax-free inks are also required for UV or aqueous-coated print jobs.

Opaque ink
Process inks are transparent, so for printing on coloured stock an opaque white is added to the ink formulation. This minimises the effect of the base stock's colour on the ink colour.

Fluorescent ink
Special inks that produce bright and vivid colours (see page 102).

Metallic ink
Inks containing metallic particles to appear like metal, such as silver, gold and copper. Metallic inks may tarnish or scuff, so it may be necessary to apply a protective varnish. Note that the metallic particles in these inks can cause contamination following final disposal of the printed piece.

Pastels
Subtle, light shades of ink.

Vegetable-based ink
Inks produced using vegetable oil rather than petroleum, which reduces the amount of ozone-depleting volatile organic compounds (VOCs) released during printing.

Quick-drying ink
Used for rush jobs or where many colour passes need to be made.

FINISHING TERM

A loose leaf item or card placed within a publication but not bound into it. Inserts include mailers and advertisements, which are placed within the pages of magazines, as well as addenda, which may be added to a book or a magazine. Addenda include paper inserts that highlight errors or other inconsistencies in the text.

☛ see Binding 34

One of several computer processes used to regenerate an image after it has been resized or remapped. Image resizing is necessary when you need to increase or decrease the total number of pixels; remapping is used to correct lens distortion, to change perspective or to rotate an image. Interpolation uses known data to estimate values at unknown points. When resizing images, it tries to achieve the best approximation of a pixel's colour and intensity based on the values of surrounding pixels.

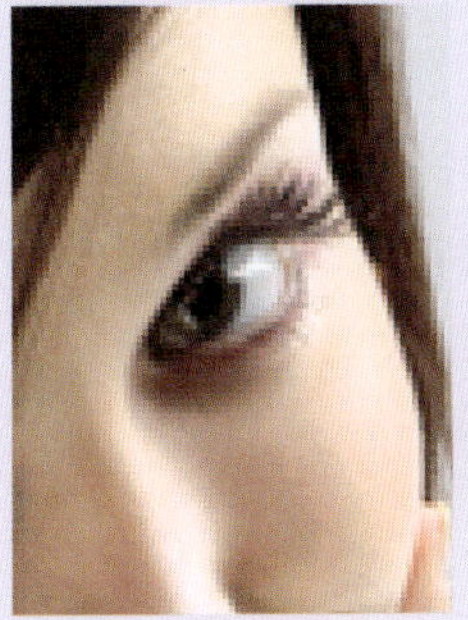

Nearest neighbour
This is the most basic and quickest interpolation algorithm because it just considers one pixel, the closest to the interpolated point, and simply makes each pixel bigger.

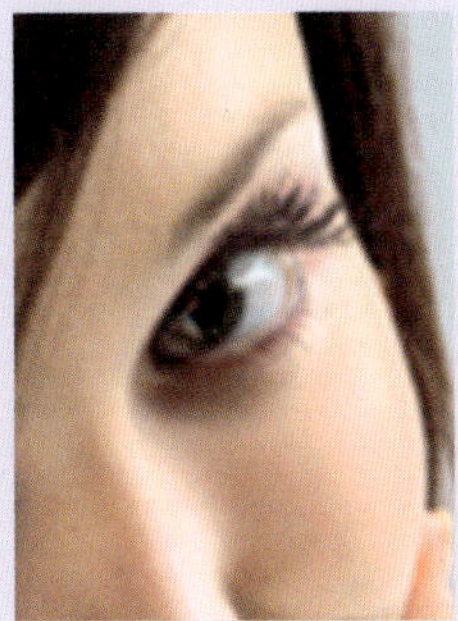

Bicubic smoothest
This interpolation algorithm is suitable when increasing image size as it offers a smoother interpolated enlargement.

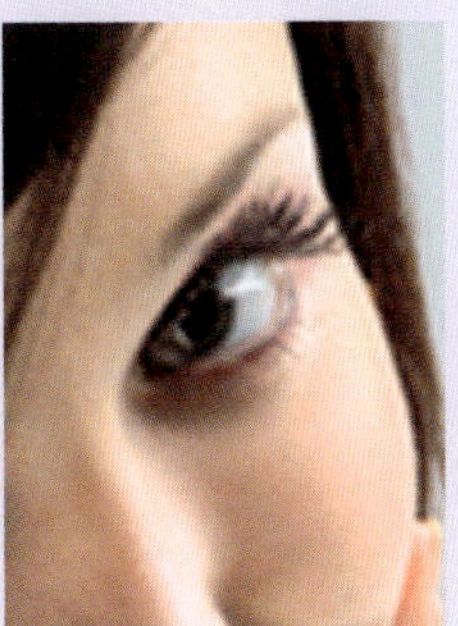

Bicubic sharpest
This interpolation algorithm is suitable when decreasing image size: it produces sharper images.

Upsizing and downsizing
It is well known that enlarging an image can reduce its visual quality as it begins to pixelate. This can be resolved by using the bicubic smoothest interpolation method. Less well known is the fact that image quality can also deteriorate when shrinking or downsizing an image. This can be resolved using bicubic sharpest interpolation.

Original image and greyscale invert
The original image (right) and the result (far right), made by inverting a greyscale.

RGB and CMYK inverts
The original image inverted from the CMYK (right) or RGB (far right) colour space.

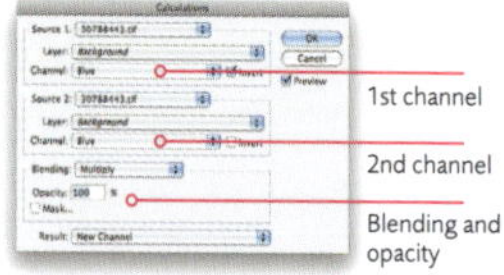

A method of changing the colours of an image to their 'opposite' colours. The result is similar to a colour film negative, but without the orange cast. The appearance of an inversion will depend on whether the original is in the CMYK or RGB colour space. A designer can also perform calculations and multiply or blend image layers to exercise greater control over the invert and produce different results.

see CMYK 54, Greyscale 121, RGB 216

International Organization for Standardization. Because it would have different acronyms in different languages the founders chose a short, all-purpose, translatable name: 'ISO', from the Greek *isos*, which means equal.

ISO has developed over 17,500 International Standards, ranging from standards for agriculture, construction, manufacturing and distribution to information and communication technologies, amongst others.

Perhaps the most significant standard in pre-press terms is the ISO paper series. The practical benefits of standardising paper sizes have been recognised for centuries and the origins can be traced back to 14th-century Italy.

The ISO standard provides a range of complementary paper sizes to cater for most common printing needs. It is used throughout Europe and most of the world except the US and Canada. The modern ISO system is based on a width-to-height ratio formed by the square root of two (1:1.4142), which means that each size differs from the next or previous size by a factor of 2 or 1/2. The AO format has an area of 1 square metre.

☛ see A Sizes 290, B Sizes 291, C Sizes 293

Jaggies

PRINTING TERM | *Also called artefacts*

An informal name for artefacts in raster images, often caused by aliasing. Jaggies are blocky lines that appear where there should be smooth straight lines or curves, often when a low-resolution image is enlarged or when the resolution of an image is changed. Vector graphics do not suffer from this problem. Anti-aliasing reduces the appearance of jaggies by smoothing them out with shaded pixels.

The image above left is uncompressed while the other image, above right, is over-compressed, resulting in the appearance of jaggies. These are particularly noticeable where the trees meet the horizon.

see Anti-aliasing 24

A technical standard used by the pre-press industry, which allows print production workflow to pass across different application domains. Job Definition Format (JDF) is an XML format that is used for sheet-fed offset and digital print workflow; web-fed systems; newspaper workflows and packaging and label workflows. JDF-enabled equipment exchanges JDF files and information about a job, determining what files it needs as input and where they are found, and what processes it should perform. Having completed its task, the equipment modifies the JDF job ticket to describe what it has done, before sending it on to the next piece of equipment. The illustration shows a typical workflow diagram for a print job, with the JDF file (the red arrows) passing from stage to stage.

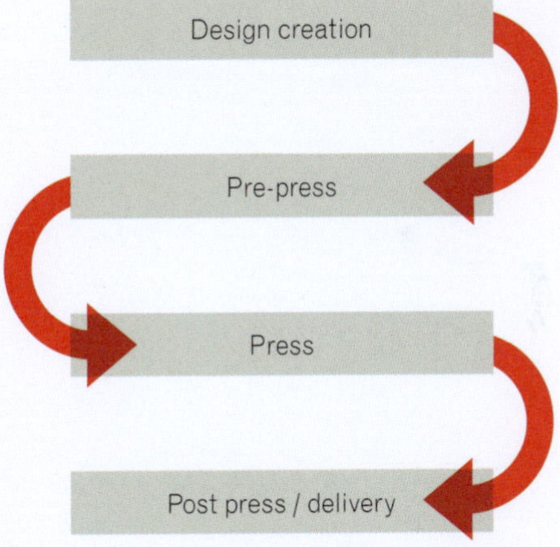

DESIGN TERM

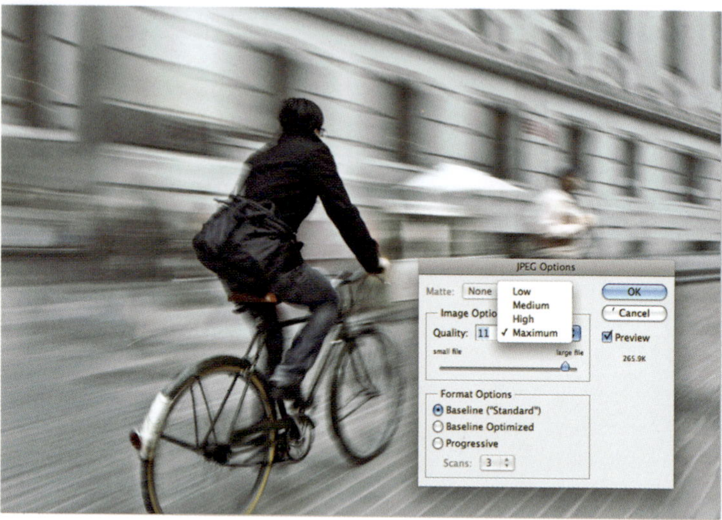

A digital file format that contains 24-bit colour information – such as 6.7 million colours, for example – and uses compression to discard image information. JPEG (Joint Photographic Experts Group) is suitable for complex pixel gradations in continuous-tone images, such as photographs. As JPEG compresses file size, image quality may suffer in printing: the image resolution needs to be at least 300ppi with maximum quality settings.

The insert shows the available options for saving a JPEG. Images are saved uncompressed to maintain maximum quality and avoid the appearance of jaggies.

☛ see Compression 60, DPI / PPI / LPI / SPI 79, Jaggies 146

DESIGN TERM

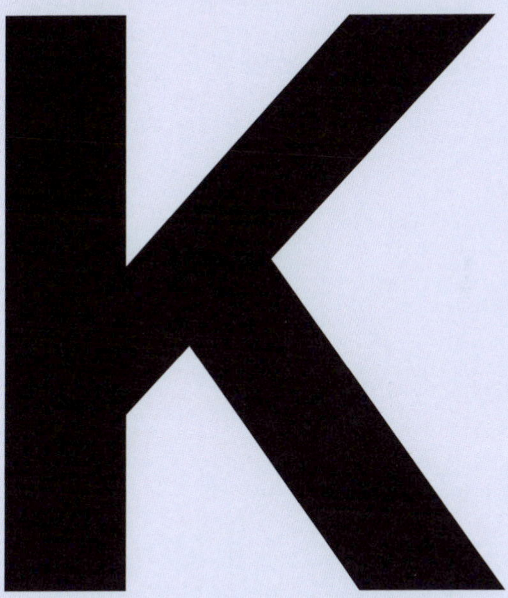

The letter used to describe black in the CMYK printing process. K stands for key: it is the colour plate that all the other colours key or register to. The use of K also helps avoid confusion with the B (blue) of the RGB colour space.

☛ see CMYK 54, Registration 211, RGB 216

DESIGN TERM

Removing space between letters to improve the visual look of a block of type. Kern originally referred to the part of a type character that extended outside its bounding block or printing block. As kerning is increased, the quantity of white space between characters is reduced. Kerning is often used with larger type sizes as these may appear loose when set naturally. This looseness can be reined in using kerning.

Start

Start

The illustration shows how some letter combinations can cause typographical problems, particularly when set at large point sizes. At the top, the s and t letters seem too far apart, while the r and t are colliding. Use of kerning and letter spacing to add and subtract produces a more even and attractive result, as the second example shows.

FINISHING TERM

A die-cutting method in which the face stock is die cut, but not the backing sheet, to facilitate the easy removal of the cut stock. Kiss cutting is often used with self-adhesive substrates to allow the sticker to be peeled away.

see Die Cutting 73, Substrate 251

FINISHING TERM

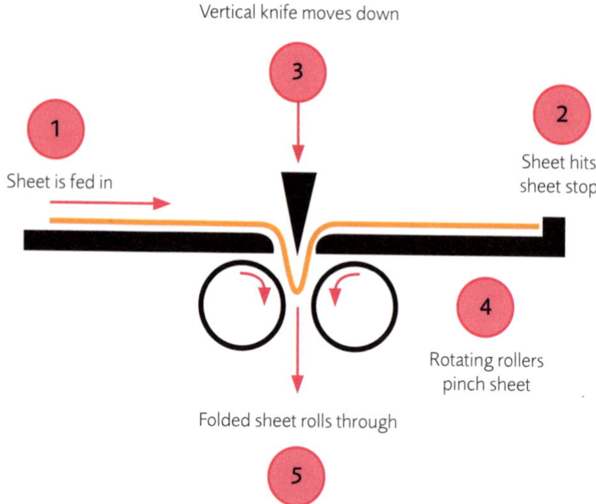

A MACHINE THAT FOLDS PAPER STOCK BY STRIKING IT WITH A KNIFE BETWEEN TWO ROLLERS. A KNIFE FOLDER CAN BE AN ON-LINE OR OFF-LINE FINISHING PROCESS. PAPER IS EITHER FED FLAT PILE, WHERE EACH SHEET IS TRANSPORTED INTO THE MACHINE BY FRICTION OR AN AIR SUCTION WHEEL; OR ROUND PILE, WHERE SHEETS ARE PULLED INTO THE MACHINE BY AN AIR SUCTION WHEEL.

see Folding 106

FINISHING TERM

A process of joining two or more different layers of material together. Laminated materials are used in print production so that a job benefits from the different qualities of the individual laminates. This may be as simple as having two pieces of the same stock with different colours. Lamination also refers to heat sealing a sheet of stock between layers of plastic with pressure and an adhesive.

Lamination helps protect a printed piece by acting as a barrier. This can prevent business cards or menus from becoming dog-eared or it can stop the foil of a foil block from wearing away.

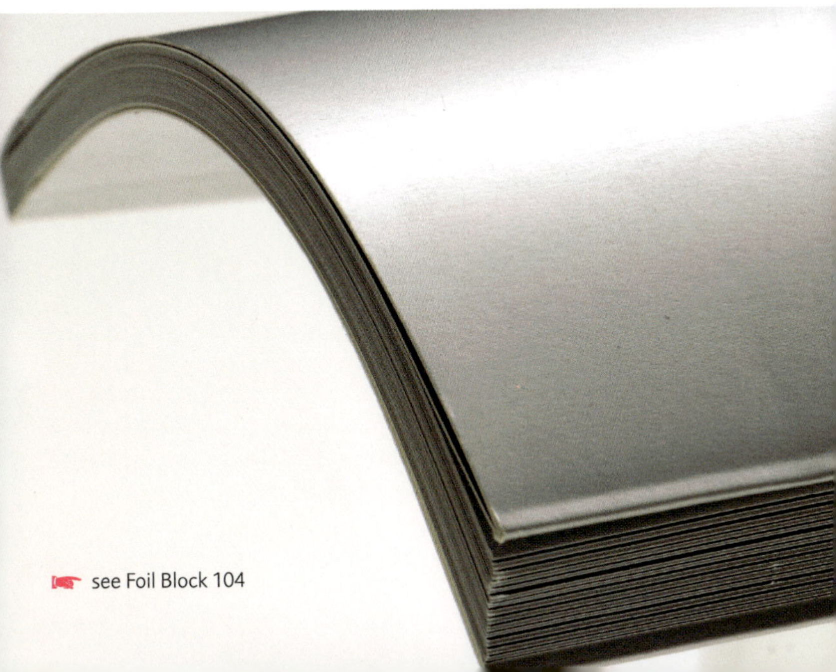

see Foil Block 104

FINISHING TERM

Shown above is a design by February London, for developer, Ipsus, which features a laser-cut print.

A print finishing process that involves the use of a laser to cut shapes into the stock. Laser cutting is similar to die cutting but it can produce more intricate shapes with a cleaner edge. Faster set-up times also mean that a quick job turnaround is possible. However, the heat of the laser can burn the cut edge.

see Die Cutting 73

DESIGN TERM

Layers

Layers, a powerful graphic design tool, are the single levels or skins of a digital image which can be worked on independently. Adjustment layers allow graphic changes to be made while the original image is preserved.

Most designs are built using layers, with type, images and other design elements created separately over a base image. This example features a distinct layering of type and a graphic intervention over the image.

Shown above are the images components that have been layered together to form the composite image, right.

see Adjustment Layers 21

DESIGN TERM

A hot-metal printing term that originates from the strips of lead that were inserted between text measures in order to space them accurately and evenly. Leading is specified in points and refers nowadays to the space between the lines of text in a text block so that the information is easy to read.

To achieve a balanced and well-spaced text block, leading usually has a larger point size than the text; for example, a 10pt typeface might be set with 12pt leading.

Text is set solid when it is set with the same point size and leading value, such as 12pt type set with 12pt leading. This may be difficult to read if the font has a large x-height.

Different fonts, however, occupy differing amounts of the em square. This can make equally-set fonts, of the same size and same leading, appear different. Some fonts occupy more of the vertical space of the em square, while others with a small x-height appear much lighter.

Computer technology makes it possible to set text with negative leading so that the lines of text crash into one another and even overlap. Text set with negative leading can look dramatic although it may be difficult to read.

see Font / Typeface 108

Part of a book or printed publication. A leaf comprises two pages, one on each side of the leaf. A leaf is typically folded, which increases the number of pages available depending on whether it has one, two or three folds, or even more. Printed page, or PP, refers to the number of printed pages contained in a book or document, as specified in the job description. It is important not to mix up these terms when specifying a job in order to avoid errors. Print jobs are specified in the number of printed pages rather than the number of leaves.

1 leaf, folded, 4 printed pages

2 leaves, folded, 8 printed pages

A leaf comprises two pages but here (left) it has been folded to give four printed pages, two on each side of the leaf. Adding extra leaves (right) increases the number of printed pages by four each time.

see Pagination 185, Specifications 239

PRINTING TERM

A relief printing method that creates a tactile depth and impression on a printed piece. Letters are set in a chase, or form, which is bonded to a printing bed. The letters are then inked and pressed on to the stock. The amount of pressure applied can be altered to create a lighter or deeper impression. Letterpress was the forerunner for modern printing and many terms associated with it are still in use today.

A defect of letterpress is also part of its quality. Each 'pull' or print will be slightly different from the prevous one as the ink and pressure levels change. Many fonts available in letterpress will not be available in digital form, which opens up creative choices to the modern designer.

see Impression 140, Substrate 251

A photo-editing tool that allows a designer to move and change the brightness levels of an image histogram. The levels command allows a designer to adjust brightness, contrast and tonal range by specifying the location of the full black, full white and midtones in a histogram. Each image will have its own unique histogram and therefore will require its own adjustments; understanding how to adjust the histogram levels enables the designer to better represent tones in the final image.

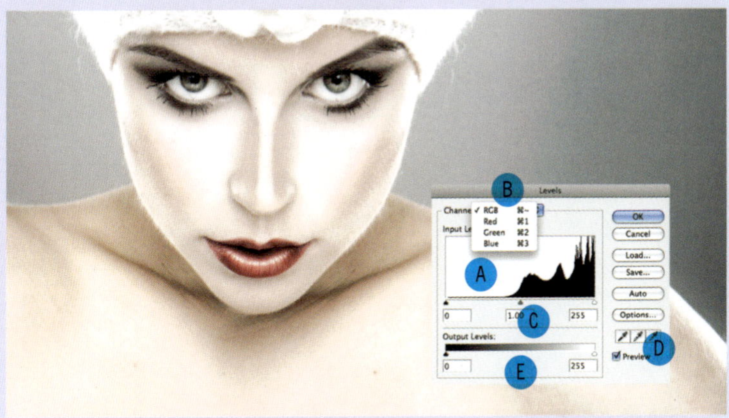

The levels are being altered in the image above. The dialog box contains various pieces of changeable information as detailed below.

A The basic histogram image

B One can choose whether to alter all channels or a single channel of the image

C Shadow, midtone and highlight values of the histogram

D Pickers sample the black, grey and white values of the image

E Shadow and highlight output levels

see Channels 52

DESIGN TERM

flag find

Encyclopædia

A group of two or three typographical characters joined together as a single unit. A ligature is used for certain character combinations that may interfere with each another when set together; common ligatures are included with many fonts, particularly expert sets. Shown above are ligatures set in Garamon, which include the fl of flag, the dotless i of the fi in find, and the ae of encyclopaedia. Shown below is a contemporary font, Mrs Eaves; it has untraditional ligatures such as the ae of encyclopaedia, which joins the a loop to the e crossbar, as well as the gi, it and st.

girl grit stag

Encyclopædia

see Expert Sets 93

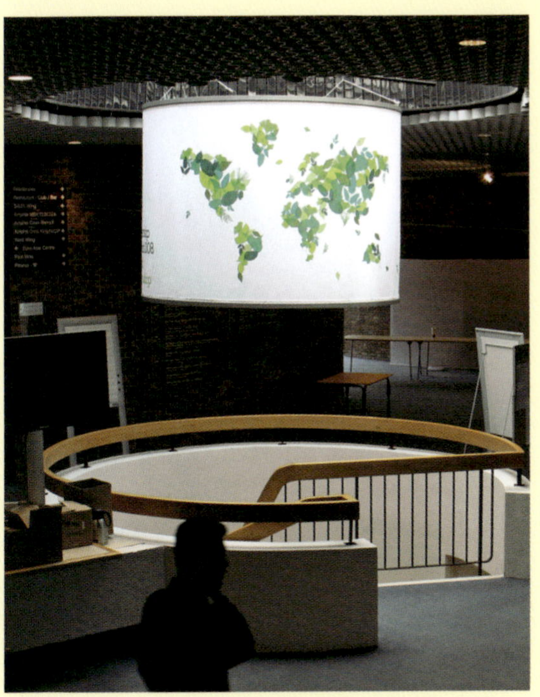

A source of light against which artwork is viewed. A lightbox is a fundamental tool for picture editors and designers: it illuminates negatives and transparencies allowing their detail and tonal nuances to be seen. A lightbox can also be used to display artwork, so it may be seen to full effect. Pictured is a lightbox and world map design created by NB: Studio for Inseed.

see Transparencies 264

DESIGN TERM

A MONOTONE DRAWN IMAGE COMPOSED OF SOLID LINES. TONAL VARIATION IS ACHIEVED BY HATCHING USING LINES OF DIFFERENT WIDTHS. A LINE ART IMAGE TYPICALLY SACRIFICES DETAIL IN ORDER TO PRODUCE A CLEAR VISUAL OF ESSENTIAL INFORMATION.

Pictured is a line art image created by Gavin Ambrose as a visual identity for fine furniture maker Fleming & Howland.

see Mono Printing 171

PRINTING TERM

A relief printing method that involves cutting an image into a substrate such as lino, which is then inked and pressed against another substrate to transfer the image. A lino cut typically produces a monotone image that has a distinctive look of coarse cut lines and hatching.

A lino cut, made by sketching an image on to a piece of lino and removing the negative space areas, leaving the positive areas to print.

see Substrate 251

Loose Leaf

FINISHING TERM

A SHEET OF PAPER FROM A NOTEBOOK THAT IS TYPICALLY PERFECT BOUND USING ADHESIVE, WITH A HARD BOARD AT THE BACK AND A LIGHTWEIGHT STOCK ON THE FRONT; THIS ALLOWS THE SHEETS TO BE EASILY REMOVED. LOOSE LEAF PAGES ARE OFTEN PERFORATED SO THAT THEY CAN BE STORED IN BINDERS OR LEVER-ARCH FILES. LOOSE LEAF PAPER OFTEN HAS RULED BLUE LINES AND A PINK MARGIN.

THE ABOVE EXAMPLE, BY STUDIO MYERSCOUGH, IS A SERIES OF LOOSE LEAF PADS, DISTRIBUTED AT AN EXHIBITION. THE 'TEAR AWAY' NATURE OF THE PRINTED PIECE MAKES A STRONG GRAPHIC STATEMENT.

☛ see Paper 187, Perforation 193

Pronounced loop, from the French loupe, *for magnifying glass* PRINTING TERM

A magnifying device used to check the quality and detail of images in photographic contact sheets and transparencies, as well as the print quality of proofs. A loupe typically has 8x magnification and is held to the eye, directly over the image being reviewed.

Choosing a loupe

There are different types of loupe available. Collapsible loupes (right) fold away and are useful to have in your pocket when visiting a printer. Standard loupes (left) are more usually kept in one location such as on the lightbox or desktop.

TIP

There is no point using a loupe if you do not keep it clean. Also, make sure you take your own loupe when press-passing; it not only makes you look more professional, it also ensures a consistent appraisal of the images you are looking at.

PRINTING TERM

Adjusting the ink film thickness to bring the colour intensity up to the correct level. Make readies are compared against a match proof to gauge when the colour level is correct. Once the print run proper commences, a note is placed among the output copies to separate the make readies from the final prints.

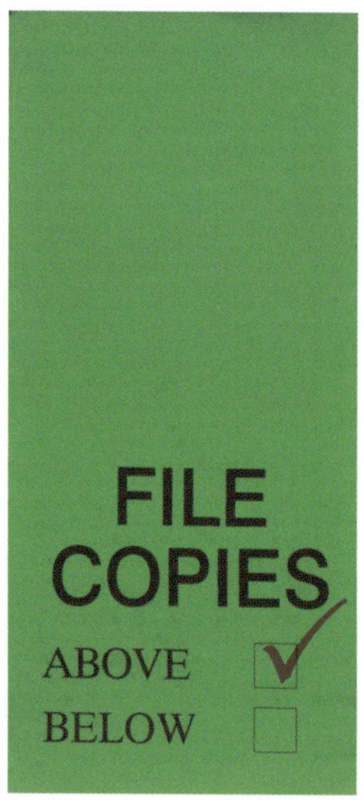

Pictured is a slip that is inserted in the print run to indicate the separation point between the make readies and the prints.

The length of a line of text.

If a measure is too great in relation to typesize, the text will become difficult to read. The same applies if the measure is too small.

To calculate a comfortable measure

The simplest way of doing this is to specify the number of characters in a line. As a general rule there should be no less than 25 and no more than 75 characters in a line; so for example, 40 characters (which is considered optimum for reading) allows for around six words of six characters per line.

Another method uses the length of the lowercase alphabet. Set the alphabet in a given typesize (A), measure it (B) and multiply it by $1^1/_2$–2 to give a comfortable setting for that typesize (C). But remember: if you change the typesize or font you will need to redo the calculation.

A
Lowercase alphabet set at 12pt type:

abcdefghijklmnopqrstuvwxyz

B
Width multiplied by $1^1/_2$–2:

abcdefghijklmnopqrstuvwxyzabcdefghijklmnopq

C
This value gives a guide to a comfortable measure that will be easy to set and read.

SCREEN TERM

A list of clickable options displayed on a screen and used to navigate a website or other digital media. Web menus are typically displayed horizontally across the top of a page or vertically down the side. They may be fixed to a specific location on a webpage, or floating so that they continue to be viewed as the user scrolls down the page. Menu sub-options can be accessed by clicking on the main option or via pull-down menus that are activated by rolling over a menu option.

When scanning a page, the eyes tend to move in a F pattern. The eye typically starts at the top left of a page and moves across to the right. It then moves down the page and moves across to the right again. For webpage design, this means it is logical to place a menu either on the left or at the top of the page.

see Scrolling 224

Interference patterns caused by the printing of colour halftone dots when the screen angles have not been properly set.

see Screen Angles 222

SCREEN TERM

For graphic design it is important to choose an appropriate monitor, with adequate resolution and size, to enable the designer to work comfortably. Graphic designers typically colour calibrate their monitors so that they accurately display colours, such as those contained in colour swatch books.

Like desk space, a monitor quickly fills due to the multiple 'command' panels of the software programs. The workstation below, in Research Studios, London, has two monitors; this allows the designer to have ample room for creativity on one monitor, while other applications can be viewed on the second.

see Colour Calibration 56

PRINTING TERM

The printing of a design in a single colour. Mono printing is typically chosen because of budgetary constraints but, while it has just one colour pass, it can still be used creatively. Methods include the use of colour stock and tints to create colour variation.

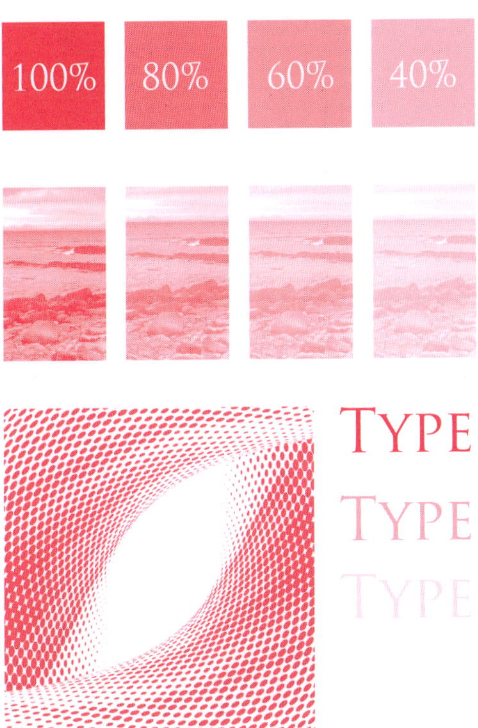

Any printing ink can be printed in tints or increments of 10% to give a stronger or weaker colour presence. The strength of a tint can make a dramatic statement in an image. A tint can be used to create a surprint, where two elements that print on top of one another are tints of the same colour. Tints below 10% may not print accurately or be very visible. To see how tints will appear on the final job, a tint bar can be printed in the trim edge of the wet proof.

see Halftone 126, Proofs 206, Tint 260

DESIGN TERM

An ink formed of two or more process or hexachrome colours. The process colours are mixed in various proportions to create the new colour. Multi-ink colours can be named and saved so that they can be used consistently across a job.

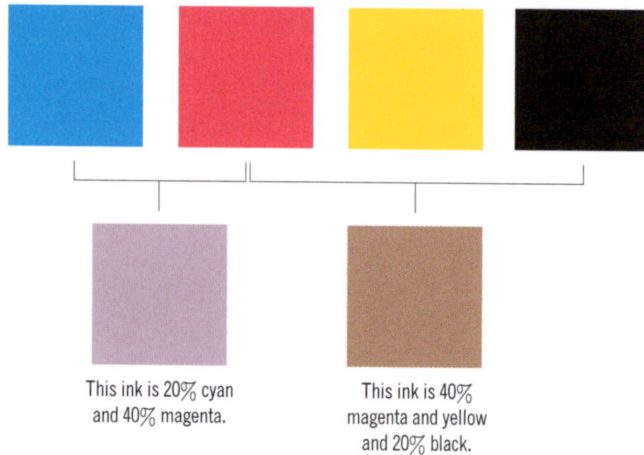

This ink is 20% cyan and 40% magenta.

This ink is 40% magenta and yellow and 20% black.

Avoid combining process inks that have total values of more than 260: it produces muddy colours, such as those below.

see Hexachrome 130

N NCR (No Carbon Required)

Also known as carbonless paper PRINTING TERM

A multiple-part, stain-free copy paper. NCR uses a dye released by contact pressure, such as writing or striking typewriter keys, to leave a permanent mark. NCR is used in various stationery applications such as order pads and receipt pads.

PRINTING TERM

A paper stock made primarily of mechanically ground wood pulp. Newsprint is a cheap stock used for high-volume printing with most of the typical printing processes but it has a shorter lifespan than other paper grades. Its low quality, rough surface and comparatively high absorbency mean its image reproduction capacity is mediocre compared to other stocks.

see Printing 200, Stock 246

Characters that represent numbers. Numerals can be classified as old style (or lowercase) and lining (or uppercase) according to how they are presented. These two different styles reflect the ways in which numerals are used in text, such as in text blocks or tabular form. Lining numerals are aligned to the baseline and are of equal height, whereas old-style numerals are not, which means that they can be difficult to read. Lining numerals also have fixed widths, allowing for better vertical alignment in tables. Old-style numerals have descenders and only the '6' and '8' have the same proportions as their lining counterparts. As lining numerals align vertically, care needs to be taken in situations where this is not appropriate, such as when dates are written. Old-style numerals are used in running text for dates (1973, for example): the characters function more like letterforms because they have descenders. The same date set in lining figures (1973) is much more prominent, which may be undesirable in body text. The numerals of sans serif fonts generally align to the baseline while those of serif fonts normally do not. Expert sets provide numerals with an exaggerated form.

1234567890

Sans serif fonts usually sit on the baseline

1234567890

Serif fonts often have descenders that dip below the baseline

1234567890

Non-aligning numerals have descenders that pass below the baseline and ascenders that reach above the x-height

see Baseline Grid 30, Expert Sets 93

FINISHING TERM

A signature produced from a sheet that has been folded three times to produce eight leaves and 16 pages; or a book produced from such signatures. An octavo signature is folded vertically, horizontally and then vertically. In folding machines, the top edge is perforated between pages 12 and 13 after the second fold so that the air can escape. The page size of an octavo signature varies according to the size of the sheet, as shown below.

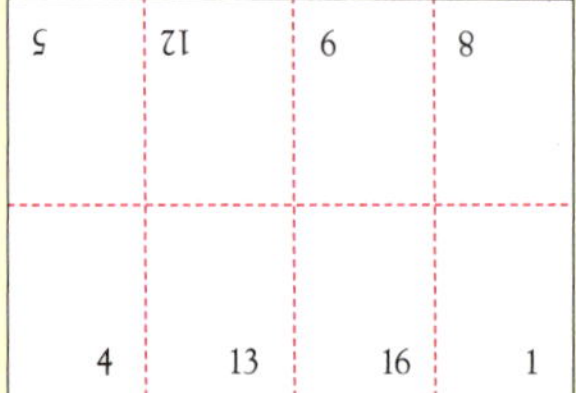

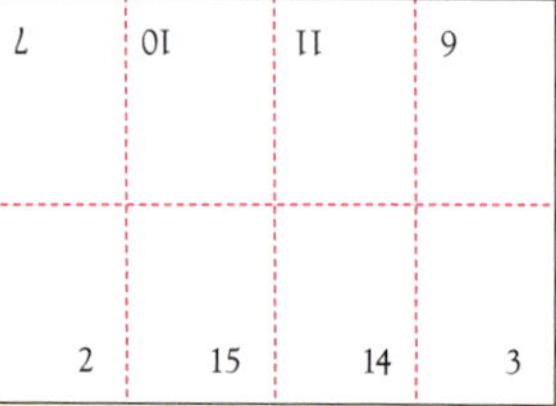

The first fold is vertical.

The second fold is horizontal.

The final fold is vertical to produce the signature, which is then cut at the top.

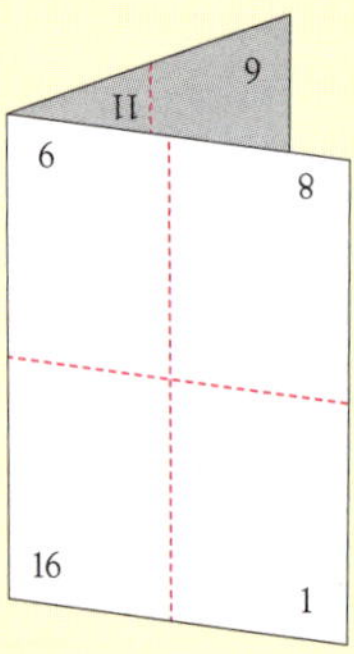

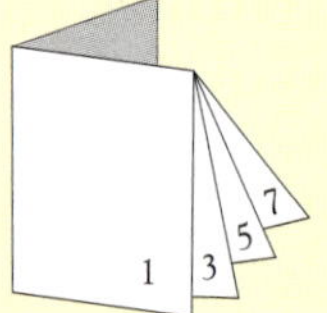

see Signatures 234

PRINTING TERM

A printing process that involves transferring (offsetting) an inked image from a planographic or flat printing plate on to a rubber blanket roller, which is then pressed against the substrate. Lithography produces good photographic reproduction and fine linework on a variety of stocks. The printing plates are easy to prepare and high speeds are achievable, which help make it a low-cost printing method. Offset lithography is available in sheet-fed printing presses and continuous web presses. Sheet-fed presses are used for lower production runs such as flyers, brochures and magazines, while web printing is used for high-volume print jobs such as newspapers, magazines and reports. The high set-up costs for offset lithography mean that it may not be the most economic choice for small print runs.

see Plate 196, Printing 200, Sheet Fed 231, Web Offset Printing 279

DESIGN TERM

The degree to which a paper stock allows light to pass through. High opacity means that what is printed on one side of a piece of stock will not be visible on the other side. Opacity is increased during the paper production process by using mineral fillers such as kaolin clay. Higher-quality printing papers tend to have higher opacity.

Opacity is also used to describe the degree to which the different layers in electronic images show through, which is stated as a percentage. The example below shows two distinct images merged together. The opacity of the background surrounding the model has been reduced to allow the cityscape to show through.

see Paper 187, Showthrough 233

A scalable format for computer fonts, first developed by Microsoft Adobe Systems. OpenType has cross-platform compatibility, so the same font files can be used on Macintosh and Windows computers, and can support widely expanded character sets and layout features. OpenType fonts containing PostScript data have an .otf file extension, while TrueType-based OpenType fonts have a .ttf file extension.

OratorStd.otf	OpenType font
OCRAStd.otf	OpenType font
NuevaStd-CondItalic.otf	OpenType font
NuevaStd-Cond.otf	OpenType font
NuevaStd-BoldCondItalic.otf	OpenType font
MyriadPro-Semibold.otf	OpenType font
MyriadPro-Regular.otf	OpenType font
MyriadPro-Cond.otf	OpenType font
MinionPro-Regular.otf	OpenType font
MinionPro-It.otf	OpenType font
LetterGothicStd.otf	OpenType font
MyriadPro-Bold.otf	OpenType font

Shown above are OpenType fonts.

PlantagenetCherokee.ttf	Windows TrueType font
TypoAmericanCom.ttf	Windows TrueType font
NewsGotDCDLig.ttf	Windows TrueType font
NewsGotDCDReg.ttf	Windows TrueType font
PORCELAI.TTF	Windows TrueType font
NewsGotTBol.ttf	Windows TrueType font
NewsGotTDem.ttf	Windows TrueType font
NewsGotTMed.ttf	Windows TrueType font
NewsGotTReg.ttf	Windows TrueType font
FerroRosso.ttf	Windows TrueType font
NewsGotTLig.ttf	Windows TrueType font

Shown above are Windows TrueType fonts.

DESIGN TERM

Typographical errors that detract from the visual appearance of a block of text.

Orphans

The final one or two lines of a paragraph, which are separated from the rest of the paragraph at the point where it breaks to form a new column. Orphans should be avoided at all costs. See the text column opposite, which has an orphan circled in red. Generally, the removal of orphans requires text to be pulled back to previous lines or pushed forward to fill the line out, although more text is often needed to alleviate the problem.

Widows

A lone word at the end of a paragraph or text column. This text column has a widow underlined in red. Generally, range-right text creates fewer widows, but to remove them requires text to be pulled back to previous lines or pushed forward to fill the line out.

Also called OM

DESIGN TERM

Text that does not fit into the space available. Overmatter is a common occurrence in graphic design and is usually solved by an editor reducing and rewriting the text to fit the space available. A designer can also reduce the font size so that the text fits, although this results in a compromised design. Overmatter is left on the pasteboard, as illustrated here, for the editor to

review, or a temporary page is created at the end of the document to contain all overmatter.

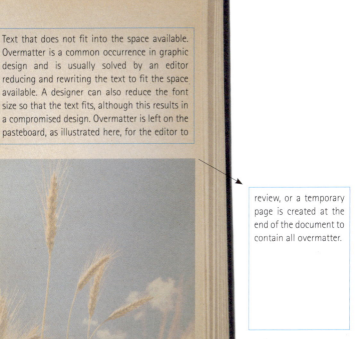

PRINTING TERM

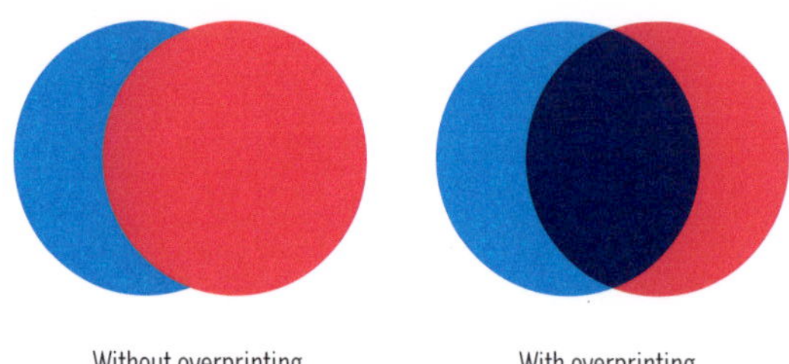

Without overprinting   With overprinting

The printing of one ink over another to create different colours. Overprinting can be used for creative effects and to extend colour options when printing with a limited range, such as two colours. The illustration above shows two colours without overprinting (left) and with overprinting (right). Notice how the two colours create a third colour when they overprint. In this instance, the new colour is blue. According to colour theory, overprinting pairs of the three subtractive primary CMY process colours produces additive primary colours. To overprint effectively, a designer needs to bear in mind the order in which the process colours print. If printing in the order cyan, magenta, yellow and black, the yellow cannot overprint cyan, for example. Blacks with different tones and intensities can also be achieved with overprinting.

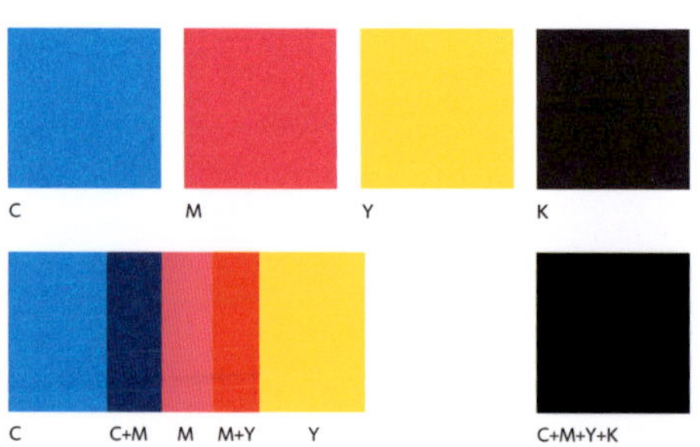

The top row of swatch chips shows each of the subtractive CMYK primary colours. The bottom row shows magenta overprinting cyan to create blue, and yellow overprinting magenta to create red. The final swatch chip shows a four-colour black. Notice how it has a deeper, more intense colour than the single colour black above it.

The empty space that surrounds the content on a printed page or webpage. On a printed page, padding is the space between columns and images. A page can be specified in one of two ways: the image columns can be fixed and padding is the available space; or the padding is fixed and the column widths altered to use the space. In digital media, padding is equivalent to the margins of a printed page, as illustrated below. The padding separates the content from the edge of the screen and helps make it easier to read.

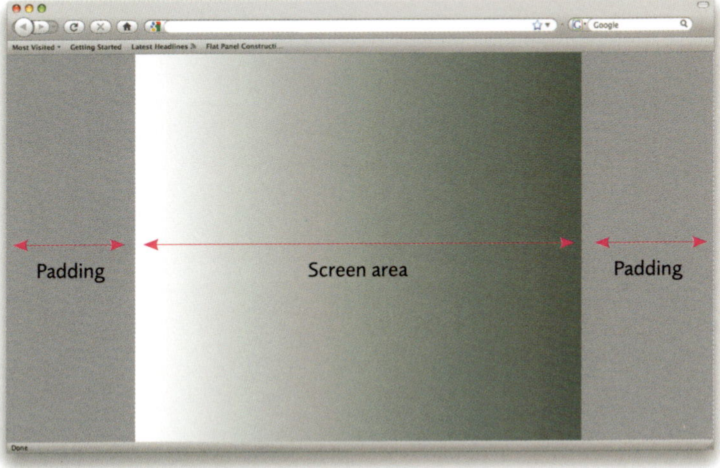

FINISHING TERM

Also called ribbon

A thin band of cloth, typically silk, which is bound into the spine near the headband. Typically used to indicate a specific location in a book, page markers reach down the entire length of a publication and extend from the tail. The example below is a book by Pentagram of their work; it features multiple markers, a subtle but effective reminder of how good their work is.

see Binding 34, Book 41

Also known as extent DESIGN TERM

The total number of pages in a printed document. Pagination is expressed as a number followed by the abbreviation pp, which means printed pages. A printed page is classed as each side of a page. For example a single leaf, folded in two, would create four printed pages.

Pictured is a brochure by Research Studios. The pagination is the total number of printed pages, even if printed on different stocks, as is the case here.

see Imposition 139, Leaves and Printed Pages 157, Thumbnail 258

PRINTING TERM

An innovative colour matching system, developed in 1963 for identifying, matching and communicating colours. A standardised swatch book of colour chips, produced in fan format, helped solve the problems associated with producing accurate colour matches in graphic arts.

Pantone Inc. produces several colour swatch books that correspond to different collections of Pantone colours. The Pantone system allocates a letter and a number to each colour: for example, m for matte and c for coated; 485 represents red. Some colours are also named, such as reflex blue.

TIP

The Pantone Solid to Process book shows how Pantone colours reproduce using the CMYK printing process. These colours can be surprisingly dull in comparison and the swatches allow a designer to see this at the design stage rather than when a job is on the press. There are two colour chips for each colour: one shows the colour printing as a special colour (on the left), while the other shows it printing using the CMYK process colours (right), with each process colour shown as a value 0–100.

1505 U

C	M	Y	K
0	61	92	0

PRINTING TERM

Feel — Form — Colour

Brightness — Opacity — Finish

A substrate that can hold a printed image. Paper has various attributes that differ from one stock to another, providing a designer with different choices and options. A designer considers these attributes when selecting a paper stock for a print job, such as visual appearance and feel, longevity and robustness, usage characteristics, foldability, image reproduction quality and budget. Environmental considerations are becoming increasingly important to designers and their clients, as they seek to make less impact on the world's resources.

☛ see Brightness 44, Opacity 178, Stock 246, Substrate 251

DESIGN TERM

The process of constructing shapes and objects from paper. Paper engineering means a designer is not restricted to using paper flat; it can be fashioned into shapes and structures. A simple folding method is a concertina or accordion fold, as shown in the example below by To The Point. Paper engineering allows information to be revealed or shown in a number of different ways as the user opens or interacts with the object.

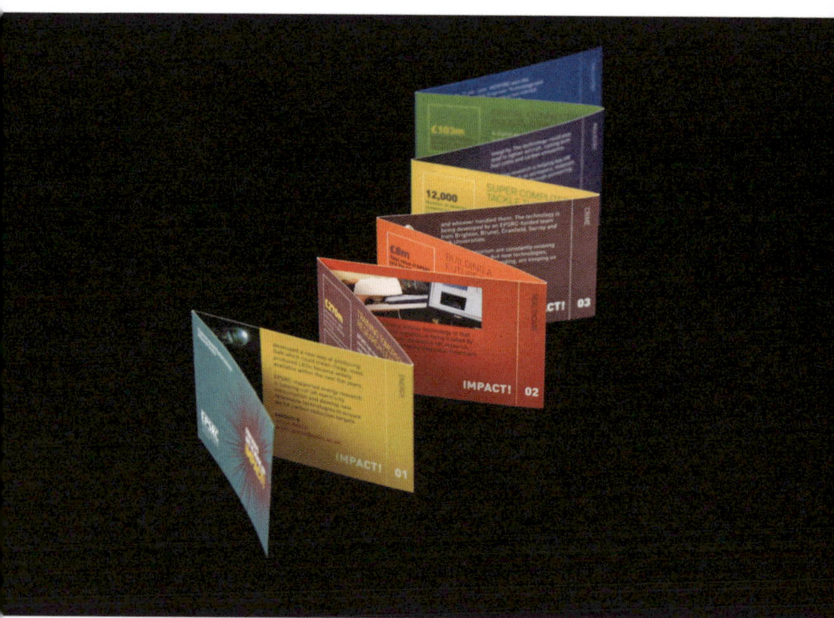

see Concertina 63, Folding 106

PRINTING TERM

The printing of a single colour, by a printing press, on a sheet of stock. The number of passes is determined by the number of colours that are to print; for example, a four-colour print job will have four passes, one for each colour. A designer typically signs off each pass when the printed colour has the required density and registration. Following this, the print run can begin.

☛ see Printing 200, Print Order 202, Registration 211

DESIGN TERM

Pronounced pas par too; that which passes everywhere

A border used to frame an image or other element. A passepartout adds a subtle decorative touch; it clearly defines the corners thanks to its contrasting colour, typically the white of the stock. A passepartout also provides a means of standardising the presentation of different subject matter.

Pictured is a spread created by Frost Design for ***CANT***, a magazine for photographer James Cant, which features photographs set with passepartout. Notice how the passepartout is an unprinted area that shows the base stock, which creates a strong contrast with the printed image.

see Stock 246

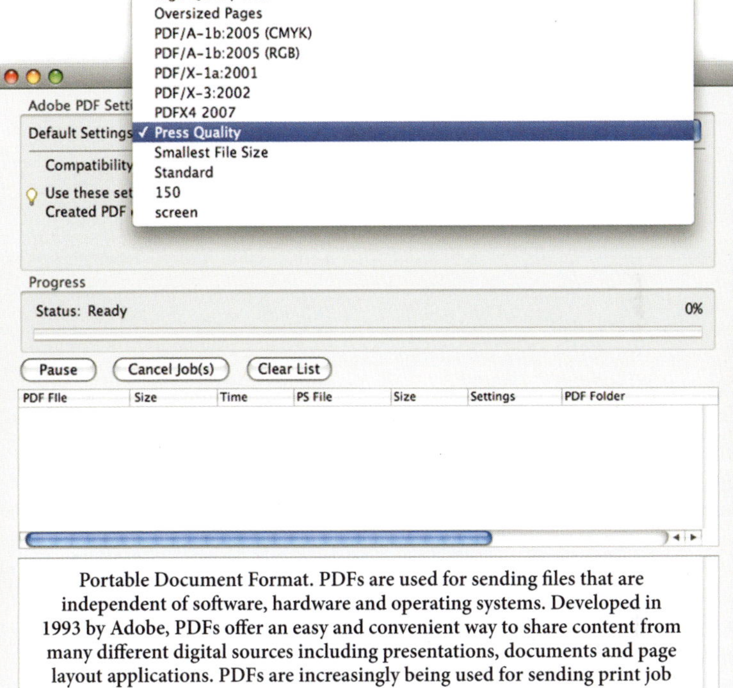

Portable Document Format. PDFs are used for sending files that are independent of software, hardware and operating systems. Developed in 1993 by Adobe, PDFs offer an easy and convenient way to share content from many different digital sources including presentations, documents and page layout applications. PDFs are increasingly being used for sending print job files to a printer.

When creating a PDF using Acrobat Distiller, a designer can determine the appropriate end use, for example print or screen. A designer can also create and save specific values for frequent use.

Perfect Binding

FINISHING TERM

A binding method commonly used for paperback books. Perfect binding sees the signatures held together with a flexible adhesive to create a spine. This adhesive is also used to attach a paper cover to the spine. The fore-edge is trimmed flat. Perfect binding is an economic binding method that produces a uniform oblong shape. However, it does not allow the pages to lie flat, which may make content printed close to the binding edge difficult to read. Designers typically leave a wider margin at the binding edge to compensate for this.

see Binding 34

FINISHING TERM

A series of cuts or holes in a paper stock. Perforations make it possible to separate parts of a printed piece, such as taking a cheque from a chequebook, a reply card out of a magazine or stamps from a sheet, such as those pictured here. Perforations are applied during printing by a perforation blade. A designer needs to indicate on the artwork where the perforations are to be located, using a suppressed colour that does not print but allows the printer to see where the perforation should go. If the colour is not suppressed, it will print as well as perforating and spoil the artwork.

see Stock 246

PRINTING TERM

Generally a dry, insoluble powder that is mixed with water, oil or another base to produce an ink or paint. Pigments are used to colour everything from paint and printing ink to plastics; they reflect specific wavelengths of light due to selective colour absorption. Pigment colour is determined by the Munsell Color System (shown below), which measures a colour by its hue, value or lightness and its chroma or greyness, which refers to its colour purity.

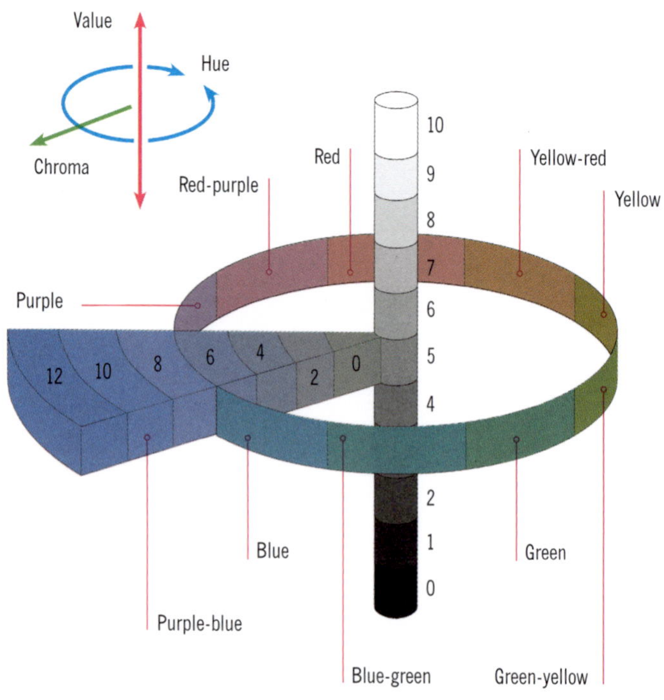

All digital images are essentially a series of recorded squares of information. Each square is a pixel. When enough pixels are placed together they form a seamless image.

In simple terms, the more pixels an image contains the higher its resolution; however, there is a note of caution here. A high pixel count doesn't necessarily mean a good image. A photograph, for example, may have a high pixel count but if the light settings are incorrect, if there is camera shake or it is out of focus, the image will be poor.

Pixelation occurs when an image doesn't contain enough information, and simply resampling the image so that it contains more pixels won't help. Certain interpolation software programs try to resolve this by predicting the colours of the new pixels following enlargement. However, there is no substitute for a good-quality original image.

Pixelation: in this half of the image there isn't enough information to reproduce a smooth tone.

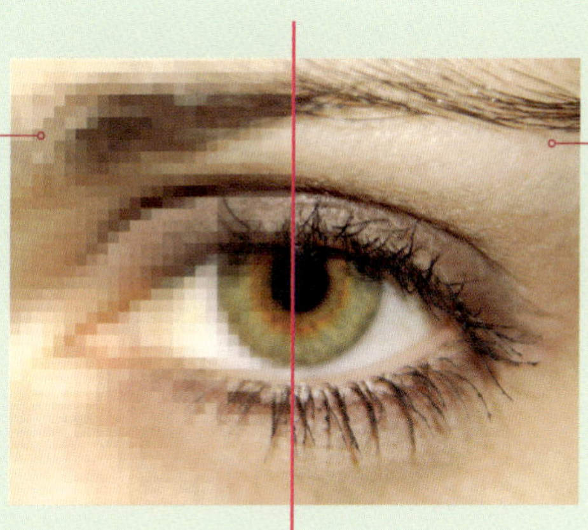

In this half of the image there is enough detail (enough pixels) to reproduce a clear tonal image.

see Resolution 213

PRINTING TERM

Used in the offset lithography printing processes to transfer an image to a substrate. Plates are typically made from metal, plastic, rubber or paper. An inked image is transferred (offset) from a printing plate on to a rubber blanket roller, which is then pressed against the substrate. The printing plate is smooth and functions on the basis that oil and water repel each other. When the plate passes under the ink roller, non-image areas that have a water film repel the oily inks that stick to the image areas. The four-colour printing process uses four plates to transfer the CMYK inks that build up a colour image. The print order of the colours can be varied, depending upon the requirements of the artwork, to achieve effects such as overprints. Varnish and special colours are also applied by a printing plate.

Four-colour image

Cyan plate

Magenta plate

Yellow plate

Black plate

Pictured above is a final image produced using the four-colour CMYK printing process. The process colour inks are applied by printing plates, which print in the cyan, magenta, yellow and black sequence to build up an image as shown. The final black plate serves to give greater depth to the shadow and contrast.

see Offset Lithography 177, Overprinting 182, Substrate 251, Varnish 274

Pictured is an original image (top) and its posterised version (bottom).

A conventional photographic technique by which the shades of grey (or colours) in an image are reduced to a specified number. Posterisation in a digital image is the replacement of the continuous gradation of tone with several regions of fewer tones, which results in an abrupt change from one tone to another. It is also a graphic effect that can be applied to an image using image-editing software.

The final review of a print job once it has been set up on the printing machine and is printing on the stock. The press pass involves comparing the printed result with the contract proof to ensure colour consistency, good registration and to check that there are no errors. Once the press pass has been signed off, the print run can begin. A designer typically uses a loupe to evaluate the printed piece and compare it with the contract proof. This process may see the designer take printed sheets outside the print room and review them under natural light in order to better judge the colour consistency.

see Loupe 165, Proofs 206

PRINTING TERM

A process that applies ink or varnish from a printing plate or screen, which contains an image, on to a substrate. There are four main processes used in the commercial printing industry: offset lithography, gravure, letterpress and screen printing, all of which differ in cost, reproduction quality and production rate or volume. Modern printing technology also includes inkjet printing, a process that involves spraying ink directly on to a substrate. Each printing process has particular strengths and weaknesses that make them appropriate for particular print jobs.

Lithography printing produces good photographic reproduction and fine line-work on a variety of stocks. The printing plates are easy to prepare and high speeds are achievable, which helps make it a low-cost printing method. Offset lithography is available in sheet-fed printing presses and continuous web presses. Sheet-fed presses are used for lower production runs such as flyers, brochures and magazines, while web printing is used for high-volume print jobs such as newspapers, magazines and reports.

Letterpress was the first commercial printing method and the source of many printing terms. The raised surface that is inked for printing may be made from single type blocks, cast lines or engraved plates. Relief printing can be identified by the sharp and precise edges to letters, with heavier ink borders.

Rotogravure and flexography are more common commercial relief print processes. They are high speed, give the highest production volume and use the widest printing presses, so they are suitable for very large print runs. Flexography was developed for printing packaging materials.

Screen printing is a relatively low-volume, slow printing method that allows images to be applied to a wide range of substrates, including cloth, ceramics and metals, which are beyond the scope of other printing methods.

☛ see Letterpress 158, Offset Lithography 177, Screen Printing 223

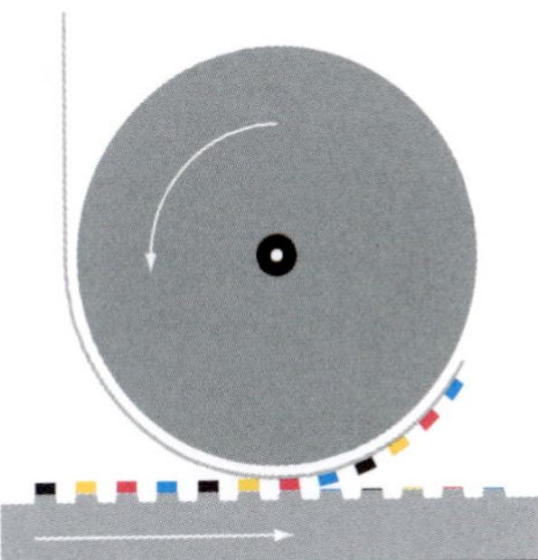

Rotogravure / Intaglio
A relief printing method that involves etching the design into a copper cylinder to create small recesses from which ink is transferred to a substrate.

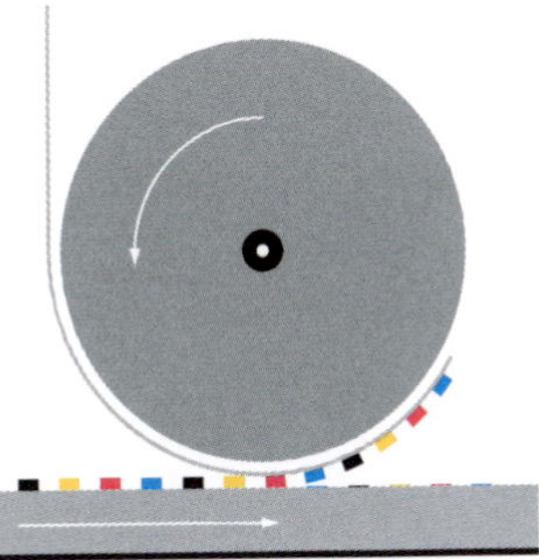

Lithography
An inked image from a smooth printing plate is transferred or offset on to a rubber blanket roller, which is then pressed against a substrate.

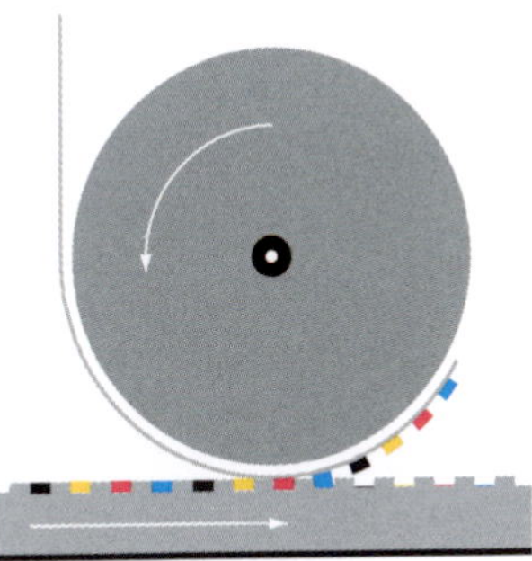

Letterpress
A relief printing method that involves pressing an inked, raised surface against a substrate.

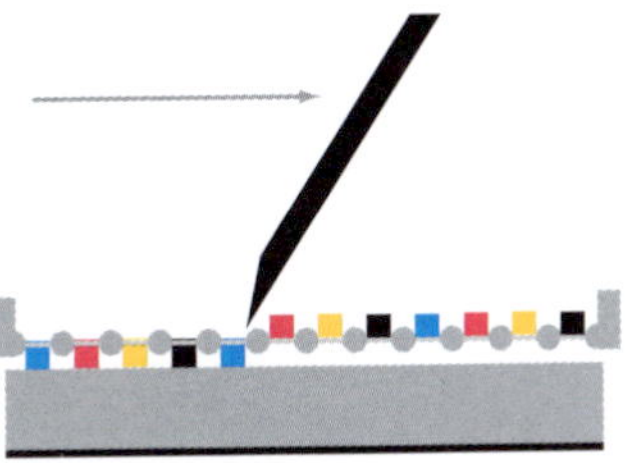

Screen printing
A viscous ink is passed through a screen, which holds a design, on to a substrate.

PRINTING TERM

The order in which the different colour passes are printed. The four-colour printing process typically prints in the CMYK order; however, a designer can specify a different sequence, perhaps to introduce a special colour or to achieve a particular colour effect, such as overprinting. Special colours are normally printed where they make most sense. Yellow may be printed last to act as a seal (printing black last can cause pickering problems that leave uneven patches on the sheet), or it can be printed first.

These are the printing plates that produce the CMYK colour passes, shown here in the CMYK order. Notice the red of the lips mostly comes from the M and Y plates.

The image builds with each colour pass, with black printed last to add contrast.

see CMYK 54, Pass 189

A print specification without a set print-run number.

Print to paper is typically specified for jobs using special paper, such as when a batch of handmade paper has been produced for bespoke invitations. The print-to-paper run continues until the paper supply is exhausted, as the cost of printing is cheap compared to the cost of bespoke paper manufacture and so the print run may as well use up the stock rather than let any of it go to waste.

see Handmade Paper 128, Paper 187

DESIGN TERM

A set of marks used on proofs to indicate corrections, which allow printers, designers, editors and their clients to communicate changes accurately and without misinterpretation. Text can be marked up or proofed by a client and returned to the designer for the changes to be made. The correctional marks are written on to a proof, both in the text itself and in the margin, so that it can be clearly seen where a correction is to be made. Although falling out of usage with general clients, proof correction marks are still prevalent in book and magazine publishing.

Margin mark	Meaning	Example
or	delete	delete delete this
	close up	make one word
	delete and close up	deelete
or or	punctuation mark, word or phrase	insert here INSERT HERE
#	insert a space	spaceneeded
eq #	space evenly	space evenly here
STET	let stand	leave marked text
TR	transpose	swap order the
/	used to separate two or more proof correction marks and often as a concluding stroke	
	set farther to the left	farther to left
	set farther to the right	farther to right
	set as ligature	encyclopaedia
=	align horizontally	align properly
//	align vertically	// align with above
X	broken character	broken
	indent or insert em quad space	
¶	begin a new paragraph	

Margin mark	Meaning	Example
(SP)	spell out	(10) lbs. as 10 pounds
CAP	set in CAPITALS	set gov as GOV
SM CAP	set in SMALL CAPITALS	set nato as NATO
LC	set in lowercase	set West as west
ITAL	set in italic	set Dylan as *Dylan*
ROM	set in roman	set *Dylan* as Dylan
BF	set in boldface	set bold as **bold**
= or -/ or ⌃=⌄	insert hyphen	multi-coloured
1/N or en or /N/	insert en dash	1981–82
1/M or em or /M/	insert em (or long) dash	Now—at last!
✓	superscript or superior	m2 as m^2
^	subscript or inferior	H20 as H_20
^ ∨ or ∨ ^	centred	centred
^,	insert comma	
∨'	insert apostrophe	
⊙	insert full stop	
; or ;/	insert semicolon	
: or (:)	insert colon	
“ ” or ‘ ’	insert quotation marks	
(/)	insert parentheses	
[/]	insert brackets	
OK/?	query to author	
⊥ ⊥	push down or work up	a stray mark
WF	wrong font	wrong font or size

see Alignment 22, Stet 243

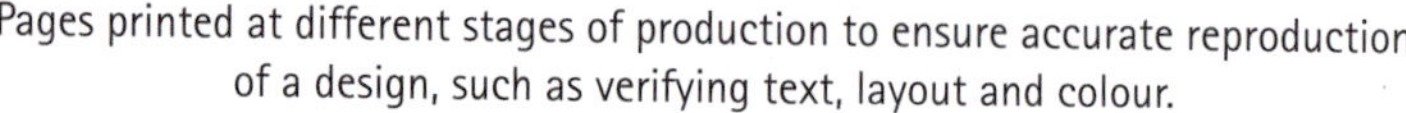

Pages printed at different stages of production to ensure accurate reproduction of a design, such as verifying text, layout and colour.

Soft or screen proof

A proof used for layout and colour information control and to check the screen structures of a print.

Laser proof

A black-and-white computer print.

Pre-press proof

An analogue or digital proof that gives an approximation of what the finished piece will look like. Includes bluelines, colour overlay and laminate proofs.

Blueline, Dylux or salt proof

A contact print produced from film.

Scatter proof

A proof of an individual photo or group of photos not included as part of the page layout.

Composite integral colour proof

High-quality proofs (such as Matchprint or Chromalin) produced using four sheets (one for each colour) laminated together in register.

Press or machine proof

A proof produced using the actual plates, inks and paper.
Also known as a wet proof.

Contract proof

A final colour proof used to form a contract between the printer and client.

A basic Photoshop document. A PSD file allows a designer to store layers containing different corrections or effects as well as the original image, as shown below.

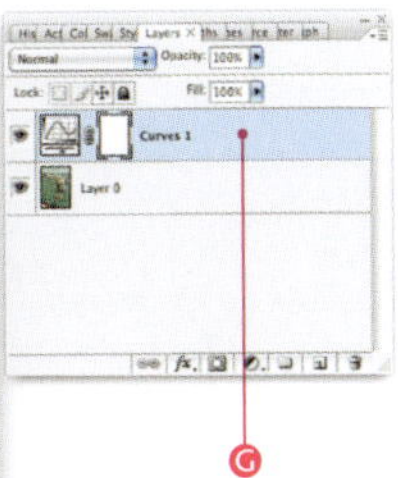

A File name

B File extension; in this case .jpg, but it could be .PSD or .TIF

C The current layer

D How many bits per channel; here 8 but can be 16 or 32

E The scale of the image view

F The document file size

G Active layer highlighted in the Layers panel

see File Format 94, Layers 155

DESIGN TERM

Any image that is composed of pixels in a grid, where each pixel contains colour information for its reproduction, such as a continuous tone photograph. Raster images have a fixed resolution and so enlarging the image decreases the quality, as shown in the detail here. Raster images are usually saved as TIFF or JPEG file formats for print and JPEG or GIF file formats for web use.

see GIF 115, JPEG 148, Pixel / Pixelation 195, Resolution 213, TIFF 259

DESIGN TERM

A file format used for storing high-quality photographic digital images. A RAW file contains a very high degree of colour information. The RAW format is a lossless format that records all the information present when the photograph was taken. Like a digital negative, you can then choose how to 'develop' the photograph. For instance, if a shot was taken with the camera set to the wrong lighting conditions – say, tungsten when it should have been daylight – the negative can be processed to take this into account. RAW files can have many different file extensions depending on the camera used, as shown below.

.3fr (Hasselblad)
.arw .srf .sr2 (Sony)
.bay (Casio)
.crw .cr2 (Canon)
.cap .tif .iiq .eip (Phase_One)
.dcs .dcr .drf .k25
.kdc .tif (Kodak)
.dng (Adobe)
.erf (Epson)
.fff (Imacon)
.mef (Mamiya)
.mos (Leaf)
.mrw (Minolta)
.nef .nrw (Nikon)
.orf (Olympus)
.ptx .pef (Pentax)
.pxn (Logitech)
.r3d (Red)
.raf (Fuji)
.raw .rw2 (Panasonic)
.raw .rwl .dng (Leica)
.rwz (Rawzor)
.x3f (Sigma)

Digital media capture is a process that creates digital images using a digital camera or scanner. Images taken by a digital camera are stored on memory devices (shown in blue here) in one of several formats.

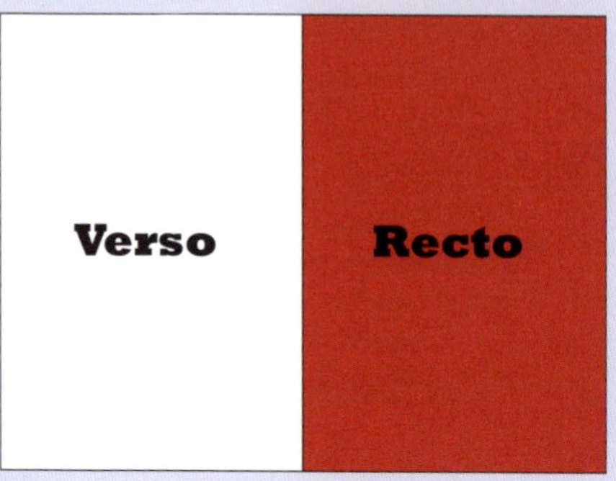

The pages of a spread in an open book. Recto is the right-hand page and verso is the page on the left. Recto verso can also refer to something that is printed front and back, with recto being the front and verso the reverse or back.

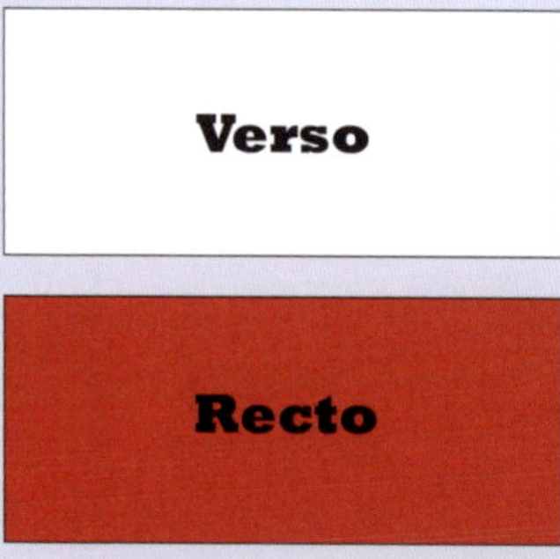

PRINTING TERM

The exact alignment of two or more printed colour passes on the same stock. A printer uses the circular dots or registration marks on the striker band to check registration and decide what adjustments are needed. One-colour printing does not present colour registration problems as there is nothing for a colour pass to register with. Misregistration is a visual fault that can make a four-colour image look distorted or blurred (as shown below). It can also mean that text is not where it is supposed to be, or that small type sizes and fine lines cannot be seen. Misregistration can wreak havoc when text is reversed out of a single colour or where colours need to overprint.

see Pass 189

PRINTING TERM *Also known as recut*

The facsimile of an existing typeface design. Remakes often introduce errors, distortions and other non-original elements that subtly change the original design.

This page is set in Mrs Eaves, a remake of Baskerville designed by Zuzana Licko. Like Baskerville, Mrs Eaves shares an overall openness and lightness, with lowercase characters having a wider proportion. However, in order to avoid increasing the set width, the x-height was reduced relative to the cap-height, and so it appears to be about one point size smaller than the average typeface in lowercase text sizes.

The term remake also applies to rectifying errors, while a job is on press, by removing elements from the plates. If there are many things that need changing, the plates may have to be remade. Remaking printing plates is costly and delays printing so various proofing stages are undertaken to ensure that this is not necessary. The sequence is:

1: author's corrections
2: correction to a proof
3: remake plates
4: finally, if everything goes wrong, reprint.

☛ see Font / Typeface 108, Plate 196

DESIGN TERM

The amount of information contained in a digital image. The higher the resolution, the more information the image contains and therefore the more detailed it is. Higher resolution also means an image can be reproduced at a large scale without a noticeable loss of information quality. Resolution is measured in pixels per inch (ppi) and is printed in dots per inch (dpi) or lines per inch (lpi).

This detail shows the individual pixels from an area of the photo.

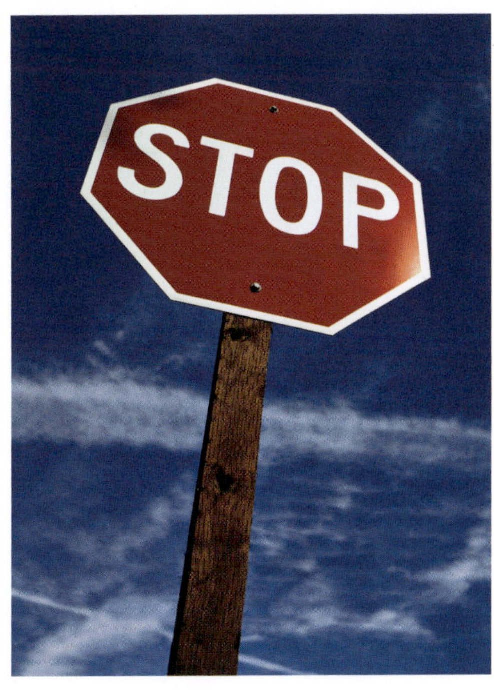

see DPI / PPI / LPI / SPI 79, Pixel / Pixelation 195

DESIGN TERM

The use of various image-editing techniques to correct or enhance photographs. Retouching is typically used to remove the appearance of perceived imperfections, such as discolouration, spots or scars on the skin of models, which would originally have been airbrushed. A healing brush was used to remove imperfections on the arm shown above. The healing brush paints with sampled pixels that match the texture, lighting, transparency and shading of those being 'healed', to blend seamlessly into the image.

see Dodge and Burn 77, Image Manipulation 138

A design technique by which the colours of a design element are switched or reversed.

Reversing images

Images are typically printed on to a paper stock. A reverse out sees a solid block of colour printed, while the image is 'removed' (above right). Fine detail in images may be lost when they are reversed out, due to dot gain.

TYPE

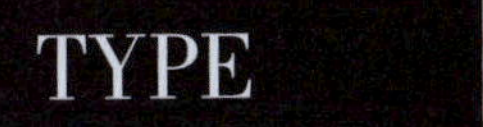

Reversing type

Reversing out type functions in the same way as reversing out images; the type is removed from a solid block of colour. Some typefaces have very fine strokes and serifs, such as Bodoni shown here, which may be lost in the reverse out. This can be compensated by increasing the typesize or weight. Text printed in very small typesizes may be lost or difficult to read because of fill-in, so text cannot be used as small as when printing positive.

SCREEN TERM

The additive primaries that produce white light when combined. The eye contains receptors that react to the red (R), green (G) and blue (B) additive colours to form the images that we see. In four-colour printing the additive primaries are reproduced using the subtractive primaries cyan (C), magenta (M) and yellow (Y).

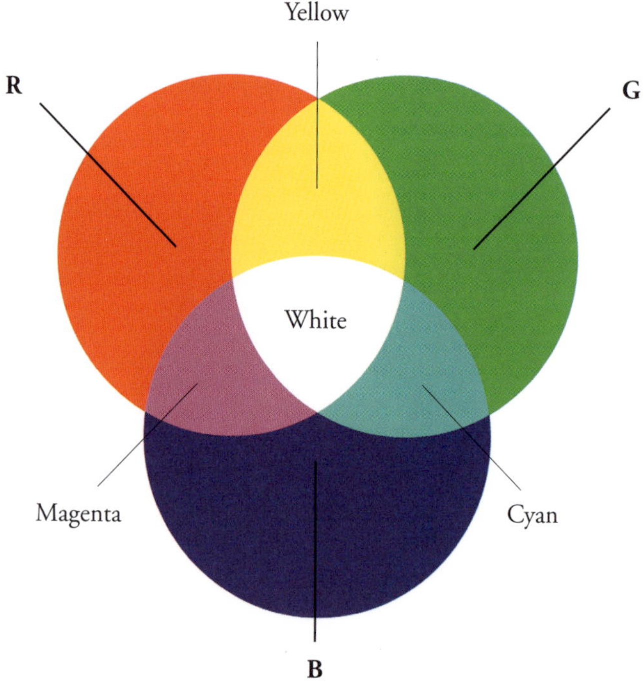

see CMYK 54

DESIGN TERM

A TYPOGRAPHICAL ERROR CAUSED BY POOR WORD SPACING, WHICH INTRODUCES GAPS OF WHITE SPACE THAT ALIGN OVER SEVERAL LINES OF TEXT. RIVERS MAINLY OCCUR IN JUSTIFIED TEXT BLOCKS, WHICH FEATURE DIFFERENT AMOUNTS OF SPACE BETWEEN WORDS. THEY CAN BE EASIER TO DETECT BY TURNING THE TEXT UPSIDE DOWN OR BY SQUINTING TO UNFOCUS YOUR EYES. RIVERS CAN BE CORRECTED BY ADJUSTING THE WORD SPACING OR EDITING AND REWRITING.

see Hyphenation / Justification 136

FINISHING TERM

A FAST AND ECONOMIC BINDING METHOD. THE PAGES ARE NESTED AND BOUND WITH WIRE STITCHES APPLIED THROUGH THE SPINE ALONG THE CENTREFOLD, WHICH ALSO ALLOWS A VARIETY OF DIFFERENT COVERS TO BE INCLUDED. SADDLE STITCHING IS NOT A STRONG OR DURABLE BINDING AS THE PAGES OF THE SIGNATURE CAN WORK LOOSE FROM THE STITCHES. ALSO, AS THE PAGES ARE NESTED, THE BIGGER THE SIGNATURE BECOMES AND THE MORE LIKELY IT IS TO CREEP.

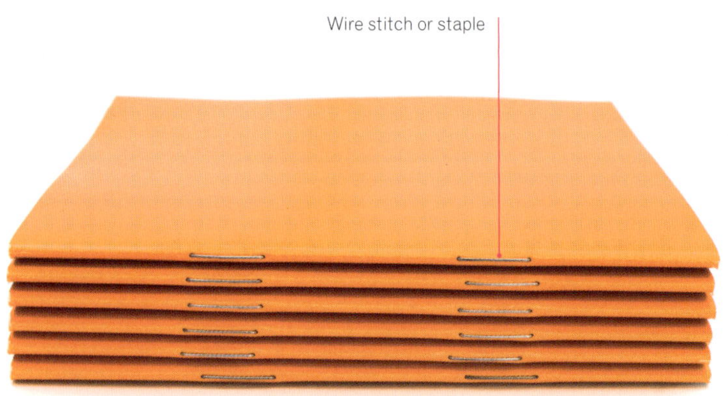

see Binding 34, Creep 68

Saturation

Also known as chroma

DESIGN TERM

The chromatic purity of a colour and the amount of grey it contains. At maximum chroma (or saturation) a colour contains no grey. Such colours are described as vivid, bright, rich, full and so on. At lower saturation or desaturated levels, the colours contain increasing amounts of grey, resulting in subdued, muted and dull colours.

DESIGN TERM

Converting an image or piece of artwork into an electronic file. An image can be scanned in a number of ways, but to ensure optimal results it is important that both the scanner and the scans are kept clean. It will often be necessary to digitally clean the scans to remove any marks or blemishes acquired during the scanning process. A good bureau will clean the artwork with a water-based solution prior to scanning and will have the scanner in a dedicated room to minimise dust contamination, which is one of the main problems associated with the scanning process.

Drum scanner
A drum scanner uses photomultiplier tubes to obtain an image. The original is mounted on a scanner drum, which is rotated before scanner optics that separate the light from the artwork into separate red, blue and green beams. Drum scanners can produce very high-resolution results from both artwork and transparencies, but they are also the most expensive type.

Transparency scanner
These can be used for scanning slides/transparencies and negatives. Transparency scanners have a filmstrip holder that allows several slides to be scanned, one after the other, in one pass. The slides and negatives must be enlarged, which means the scanners need very high resolutions, such as 4000dpi.

Flatbed scanner
The scanner features a glass plate upon which the artwork is placed. When scanning, the artwork is lit and an optical array passes underneath to read the light reflected from it. The scanners are easy to use and produce good reproduction of flat tone artwork; they have become widespread as they are cheap and often packaged with home computers. However, they have lower resolution capacity compared to other scanners, which means they are not suitable for high-quality reproduction. They also need special accessories to be able to scan transparencies.

see Transparencies 264

Also called creasing

FINISHING TERM

Creating a fold in a substrate. Scores are used to reduce the size of a piece of paper: either to make it more manageable, such as a map; or to prepare it for binding, such as the printed section of a book. The witty moving card below, by Studio Myerscough for film company DNA, makes creative use of scoring and folding.

see Binding 34, Book 41, Folding 106

PRINTING TERM

The inclination or angle of the rows of halftone dots that are printed to form colour images in the four-colour printing process. The rows of halftone dots for each colour are set at an angle to prevent them from interfering with each other when printed and causing unwanted moiré patterns. Setting the halftone dots at different screen angles ensures that they give a better coverage of the printed surface.

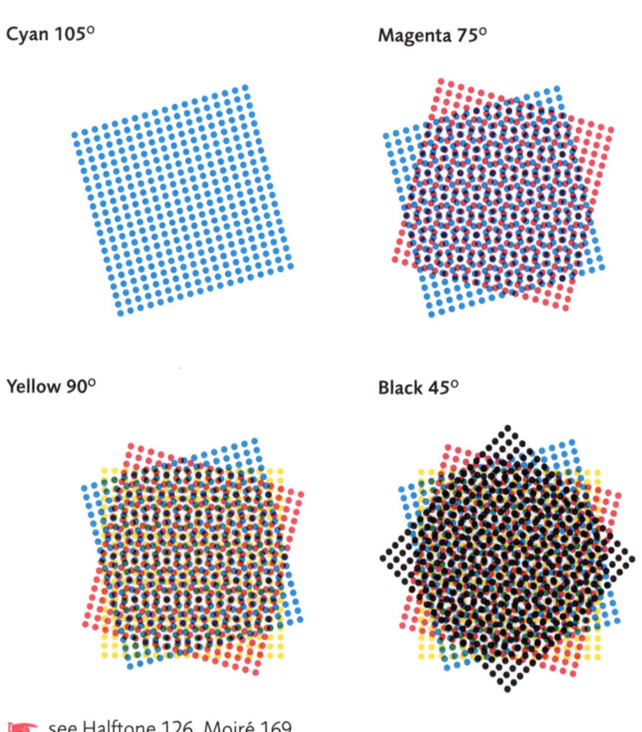

see Halftone 126, Moiré 169

Also called silk screen printing

PRINTING TERM

A low-volume printing method. Screen printing, or silk screen printing (originally the screens were made from silk), allows almost any surface to be printed, be it textured paper, wood, metal or cloth. It is a relatively slow process, and therefore expensive, but for short-run bespoke items it works very well. The process uses viscous inks, which dry quickly and form solid colours. Each colour is applied separately, so consideration needs to be given to the print order and colours used.

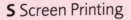

see Printing 200

SCREEN TERM

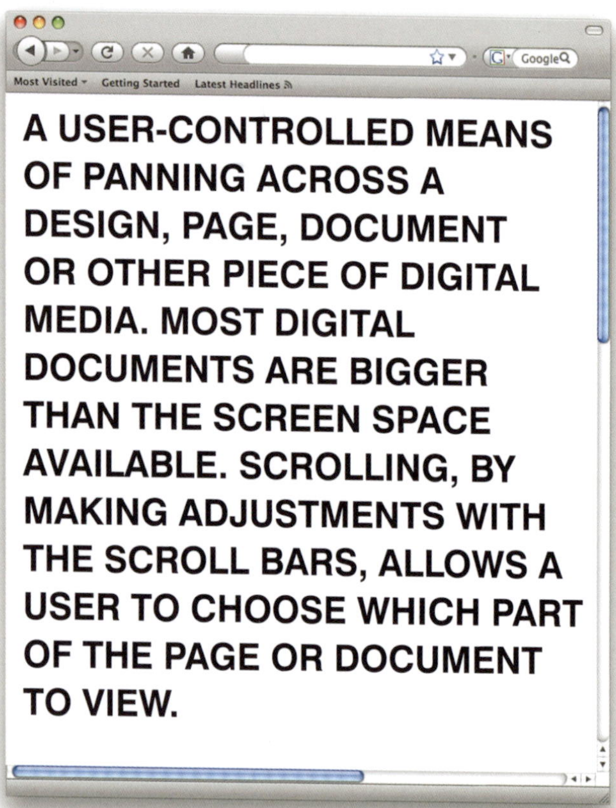
Most Visited
Getting Started
Latest Headlines
Google
A USER-CONTROLLED MEANS OF PANNING ACROSS A DESIGN, PAGE, DOCUMENT OR OTHER PIECE OF DIGITAL MEDIA. MOST DIGITAL DOCUMENTS ARE BIGGER THAN THE SCREEN SPACE AVAILABLE. SCROLLING, BY MAKING ADJUSTMENTS WITH THE SCROLL BARS, ALLOWS A USER TO CHOOSE WHICH PART OF THE PAGE OR DOCUMENT TO VIEW.

Selective colour *Meaning No. 1*

An image manipulation technique that allows individual colours to be altered independently of one another, which can be useful for removing colour casts and imbalances.

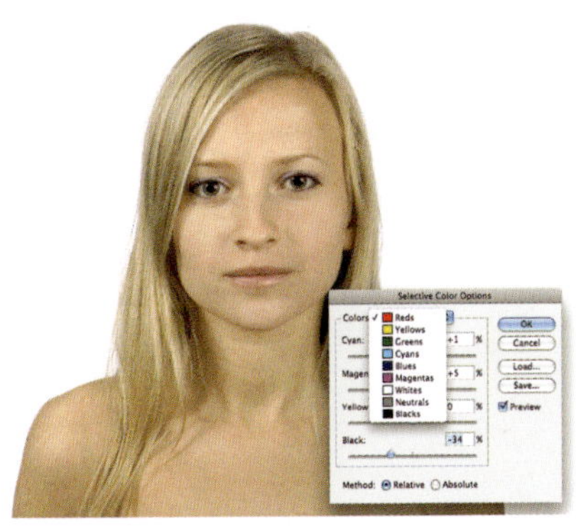

Selective colour *Meaning No. 2*

A creative image manipulation technique whereby an image is desaturated and specific areas of colour are allowed to remain, or show through.

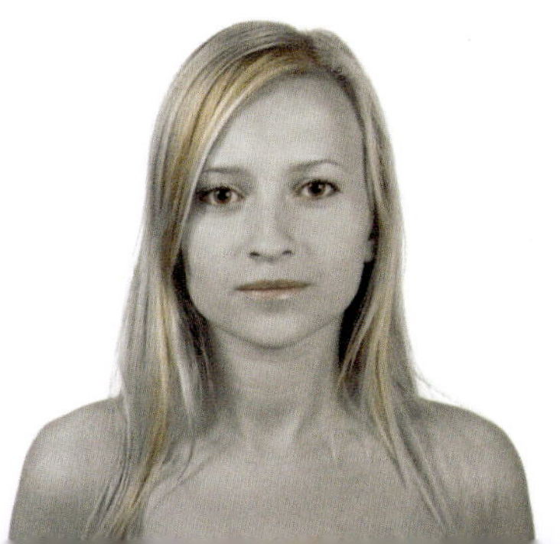

FINISHING TERM

Self cover

Where the covers of a publication are printed as part of its signatures, on the same stock and on the same passes. With a 12-page section, pages 1 and 12 are usually the covers.

Separate cover

Where a cover of a different stock or weight is printed separately from the publication body, page 1 of the signature forms the first page rather than the front cover. The signature is subsequently bound into the cover using, for example, saddle stitching.

OBC (outside back cover)
OFC (outside front cover)
IFC (inside front cover)
IBC (inside back cover)

1 2 3 4 5 6 7 8

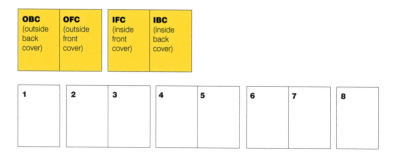

see Saddle Stitch 218

DESIGN TERM

Sepia image

Deep red

Deep emerald

Traditionally a dark-brown ink or pigment, produced from cuttlefish, used to create a tonal image or photograph. A sepia tint can now be applied digitally using a set of predescribed filters for a more contemporary feel, as shown above.

see Filters 96, Pigment 194

PRINTING TERM

The unwanted transfer of ink from one printed sheet to another. Set-off occurs when the ink on a printed sheet has not had time to dry before it comes into contact with another sheet, perhaps during folding or binding. Set-off can be avoided by the use of an anti-set-off spray powder, by using quick-drying inks or by allowing sufficient drying time. Notice how intentional set-off has transferred the image of the dog (above) to the opposite page.

THE UNWANTED TRANSFER OF INK FROM ONE PRINTED SHEET TO ANOTHER. SET-OFF OCCURS WHEN THE INK ON A PRINTED SHEET HAS NOT HAD TIME TO DRY BEFORE IT COMES INTO CONTACT WITH ANOTHER SHEET, PERHAPS DURING FOLDING OR BINDING. SET-OFF CAN BE AVOIDED BY THE USE OF AN ANTI-SET-OFF SPRAY POWDER, BY USING QUICK-DRYING INKS, OR BY ALLOWING SUFFICIENT DRYING TIME. NOTICE HOW INTENTIONAL SET-OFF HAS TRANSFERRED THE IMAGE OF THE DOG (ABOVE) TO THE OPPOSITE PAGE.

☛ see Binding 34, Folding 106

DESIGN TERM

An image adjustment technique that increases contrast to bring an image into focus. While it is preferable to only use sharp-focus images, inevitably there will be occasions when images are supplied that are slightly out of focus. Scanned images can appear slightly blurred, or digital images can have the traces of camera shake, for example. Sharpening should be applied in small increments on a duplicated image level so that you can reference the original image and then blend the original and sharpened levels to achieve the best result. If the image also contains a noise pattern it should be removed prior to sharpening, otherwise it will be exaggerated.

Original image
Original image with slightly soft focus.

Sharpened
The sharpening filter applies more contrast, creating a crisper image.

Over-sharpened
An over-sharpened image degrades the quality, although it can produce an artistically interesting result.

see Dodge and Burn 77

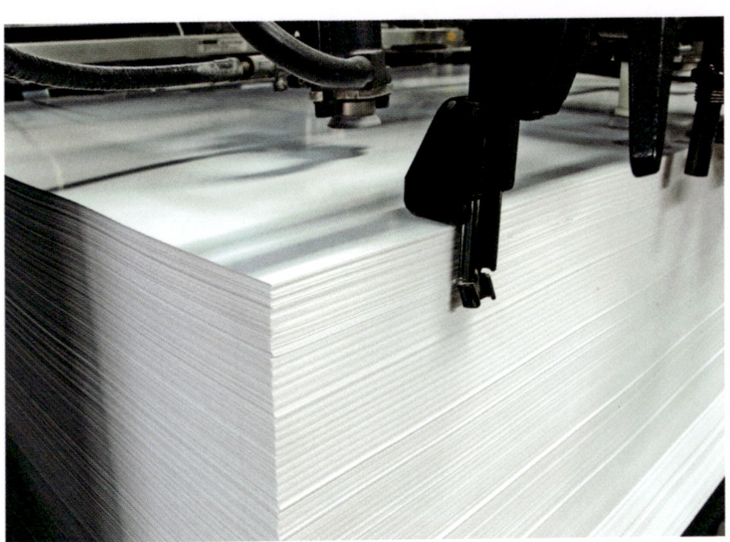

A printing method that involves feeding individual sheets into the printing press, rather than a continuous web of paper. Sheet-fed printing is used for small- and medium-sized print jobs, which do not have the print run to generate the economies of scale required for web printing. A sheet-fed printing machine is typically fed with a ream of paper at a time.

Ream
A block of 500 sheets of paper. A ream was formerly 20 quires, which was 480 sheets; one quire equals 24 sheets. A 480 sheet ream is now known as a short ream.

see Printing 200

PRINTING TERM

A method of printing a darker, richer black by underprinting with the subtractive primaries. Printing a rich black prevents bounce, a registration problem that can occur when non-colour areas print adjacent to heavy colour areas. Printing a 50% shiner of cyan, magenta and yellow produces a grey colour that covers registration errors with the black due to the shared colours. Using a shiner, flat areas of black can appear warmer or cooler. The middle panel, printed with a 60% cyan shiner, is richer and cooler than the upper panel, which is printed black only. The lower panel prints with a 60% magenta shiner and produces a warm black.

K: 100

C:60 M:0 Y:0 K: 100

C:0 M:60 Y:0 K: 100

see Four-colour Black 110

S Showthrough

Also called see through / look through

DESIGN TERM

An image or design that can be seen through the reverse of the substrate upon which it has been printed. It typically occurs when thin, translucent stocks are used, as shown above. Showthrough is generally considered an error although it can be used to good creative effect. Pictured is a design created by Mark Studio for photographer Henry Iddon, which features a stock deliberately chosen to benefit from showthrough.

☛ see Bible Paper 33, Stock 246

FINISHING TERM *Also called sections*

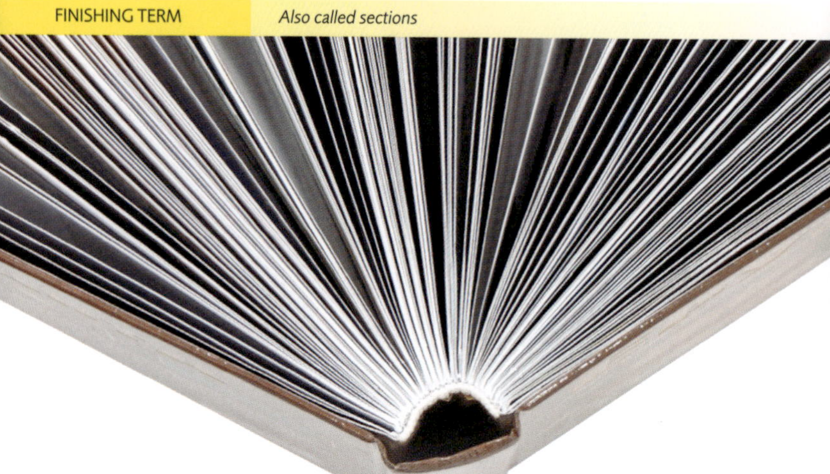

Sheets of paper folded to form several pages. A book typically contains several signatures that are gathered and bound together. The term signature refers to a letter at the tail of each section, running in alphabetical order, which enables the gatherer to collate the sections in order for binding. When planning the extent (number of pages) of a publication, a designer should bear in mind the number of pages in the signatures (16pp for example) and seek to complete the publication in a round number of signatures, rather than having to use half-sections.

☛ see Book 41, Leaves and Printed Pages 157

CAPITAL LETTERS that have been cut at a smaller size than a typeface's roman capitals. Small caps are useful for setting initialised acronyms, such as FAQS (frequently asked questions), which avoids over-emphasising it in body text.

Not all fonts come with a set of small caps, so you need to check before starting a design if you intend to use them.

The difference between real and fake small capitals is shown below:

REAL SMALL CAPITALS are created to complement body copy by having the same stroke weights.

FAKE SMALL CAPITALS alter the size but not the weight of a letterform; creating a lighter-looking set of letters that don't blend with the main body copy.

see Font / Typeface 108

SCREEN TERM

A DIGITAL SCREEN ON A HAND-HELD DEVICE SUCH AS A DIGITAL CAMERA, MOBILE TELEPHONE, MP3 PLAYER OR OTHER ELECTRONIC EQUIPMENT. DESIGNING FOR A SMALL SCREEN TYPICALLY CALLS FOR GREATER SIMPLICITY TO AID READABILITY, WITH FEWER COLOURS USED AND TYPEFACES THAT READ WELL AT SMALL POINT SIZES.

see Font / Typeface 108

Space after and space before are used to control the space between lines.

¶

We are familiar with a hard line space, as shown above. This is a full space, to the same height as the copy.

A solid space set between lines

A more subtle variation is space after, a paragraph setting that controls the amount of space that follows a hard return before the next text line.

As shown here.

A 2pt space applied after this line

This setting can also be applied to the first line of a paragraph to set the amount of space that precedes it, which therefore spaces it from the previous paragraph.

Space after and space before can produce subtle or bold interventions, as these examples show.

A 10pt space applied before this line

S Special Colour / Spot Colour

DESIGN TERM

Any colour generated by a single pass. Special, or spot, colours differ from process colours in that they are produced from a single ink rather than a mixture of two or more inks. While the four-colour CMYK printing process can produce a wide range of colours, it is sometimes necessary to use a special spot colour to ensure that a colour prints accurately, such as for a company logo. A special colour is printed solid to give a richer, more vibrant colour, rather than being composed of halftone dots. Spot colours are available in a vast range of hues and tones as specified by colour libraries such as Pantone or Trumatch. Most spot colours have a CMYK process colour equivalent that is created by mixing them in various proportions. Using spot colours is also cheaper than using process colours as fewer passes are required on the printing press. The limited gamut of the CMYK process colours also means that spot colours are necessary to print certain hues. Each spot colour requires its own printing plate and will have its own pass on the press. Spot or special colour also commonly refers to any colour produced using non-standard offset inks, including pastels, metallics, fluorescents and spot varnishes. These may also be referred to as solid colours.

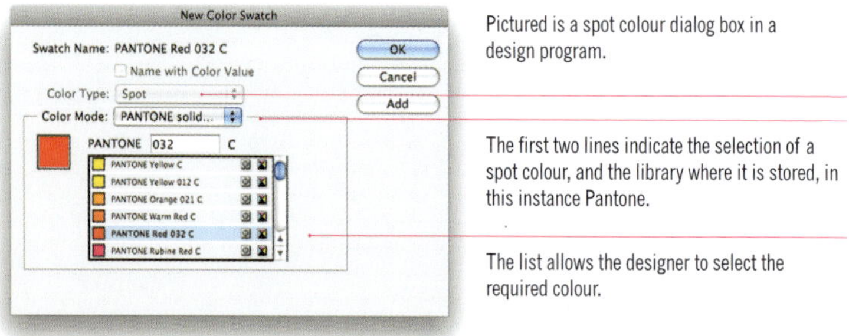

Pictured is a spot colour dialog box in a design program.

The first two lines indicate the selection of a spot colour, and the library where it is stored, in this instance Pantone.

The list allows the designer to select the required colour.

see CMYK 54, Fluorescent 102, Pantone 186, Varnish 274

FINISHING TERM

The technical requirements of a print job or order. The specification of a print job includes all the information necessary for a printer to be able to provide an accurate quotation. Once the print job has been contracted, the specification acts as the list of requirements. The print specification below shows key elements such as the paper to be used, the number of pages and colours, and the proofing and binding requirements.

Origination:	32 A4 page(s)
Proofing:	11 A2 hi-res matchprint proof(s)
Repro:	Files supplied
Finished size:	A4 Portrait (297mm deep x 210mm wide)
Printing:	28 pages + 2 gatefolds in 4 colour process throughout and machine sealed on both sides
Misc finish:	Cover 4 pages Cover silver foiled onto Colorado material, lined onto 3000mic greyboard
Paper:	Cover 4 pages 100 gsm Colorado Text 32 pages 170 gsm Chorus Silk
Binding:	PUR bind, allowing for 2 x gatefolds and attaching one ribbon marker
Packing:	In boxes, maximum of 25 per box
Delivery:	One London address

see Gatefold 113, Proofs 206

FINISHING TERM

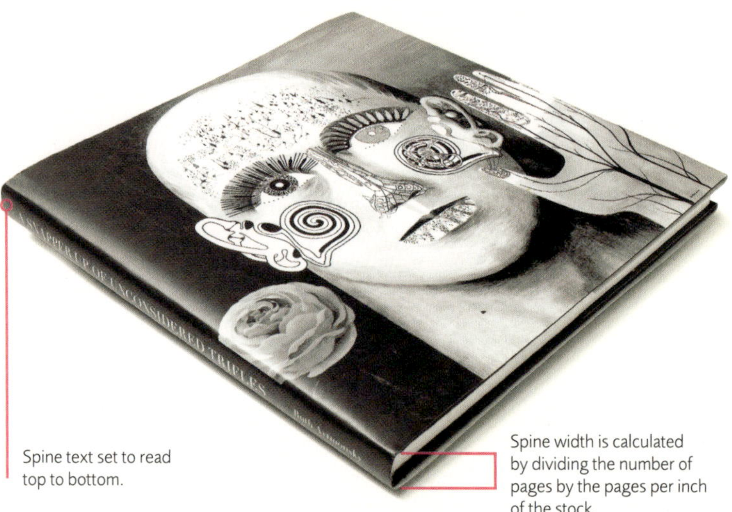

Spine text set to read top to bottom.

Spine width is calculated by dividing the number of pages by the pages per inch of the stock.

Different countries follow different conventions for the orientation of text on a spine. In the UK and US text is typically placed so it runs top to bottom, which means it reads left to right when the book is placed cover up on a flat surface. In Europe, the convention is to place spine text bottom to top.

Pictured is a book called *A Snapper Up of Unconsidered Trifles* created by Webb & Webb for artist Barbara Jones. It features spine text that runs top to bottom so it can be read from left to right.

☛ see Dust Jacket 85

Also known as a DPS or double-page spread; double-truck in the USA PRINTING TERM

The two centre pages of a signature that print as a single sheet. A signature only has one spread, nestled in the centre. Although we think of any two facing pages as a spread this isn't actually the case. The other facing pages in a signature are called *false doubles*. Artwork that passes over the pages of false doubles can be prone to misalignment (as illustrated below) caused by the folding and binding processes, so for content that needs to read over two pages, a spread should be utilised where possible.

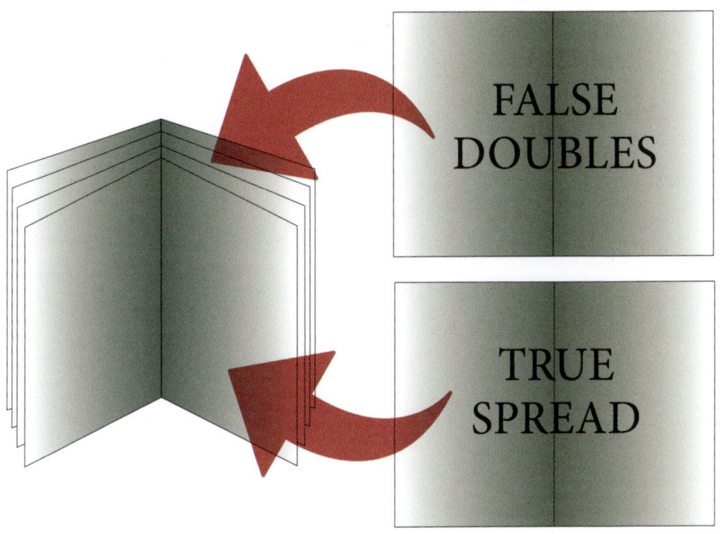

Spread also means the enlargement of two adjacent images in order to achieve good registration. See trapping for further information.

see Recto Verso 210, Signatures 234, Trapping 265

DESIGN TERM

The process of duplicating an object and spacing. The step-and-repeat command allows a designer to control the amount of times the duplicated object is repeated, as well as the distance between them, as shown in the squares above.

Step controls the distance an object moves; repeat controls the number of times an object is repeated.

DESIGN TERM

A proof correction mark directing that a letter, word or other element marked for omission or correction is to be kept.

STET

see Proof Correction Marks 204

FINISHING TERM

Book binding methods that use thread to sew through the sheets of a publication from the side rather than the spine. Sewn bound is also called stab binding because all sheets are sewn on the same pass. Sewn bound binding is rigid, strong and economical, and its pages do not lie flat. Pictured is a publication created by February Design, which features a Singer-sewn binding. Notice how the stitches run along the spine of the signature and add a tactile element to the piece.

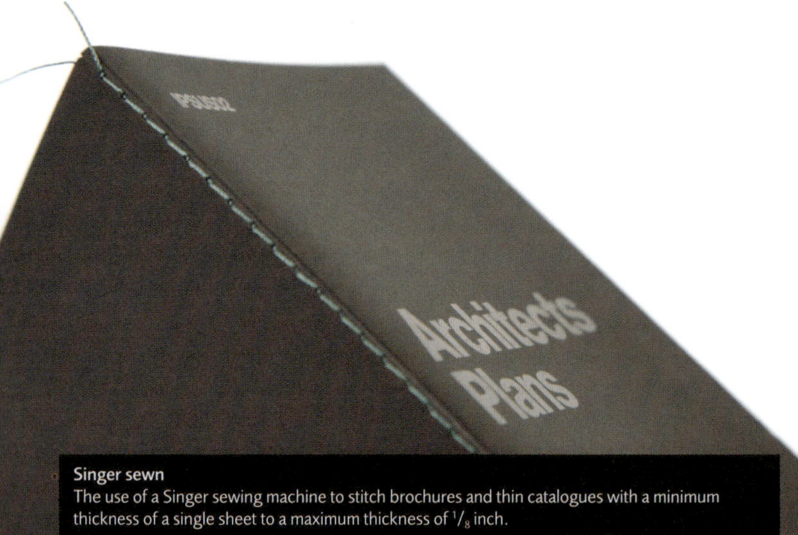

Singer sewn
The use of a Singer sewing machine to stitch brochures and thin catalogues with a minimum thickness of a single sheet to a maximum thickness of $^1/_8$ inch.

see Binding 34

Also known as frequency modulation printing PRINTING TERM

A printing method that uses different dot sizes and placement as an alternative to the traditional halftone method of four-colour printing. Stochastic printing helps avoid moiré patterns, which particularly occur with halftone dots, and it is used for fine art reproduction as the dots have little visibility, resulting in high-quality colour reproduction. Stochastic printing also allows a wider gamut of colours to be produced with additional inks, such as the orange and green of the hexachrome printing process.

Flat tint
A flat tint features uniform dots with the same size and spacing between them.

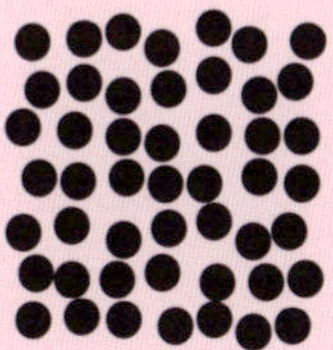

First order stochastic printing
This maintains a fixed dot size but has varied dot spacing and allows some dots to touch.

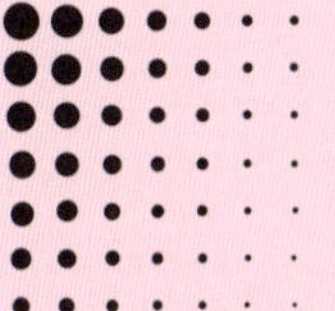

Conventional halftone
A conventional halftone allows varied dot size to give different colour tones but with fixed dot spacing.

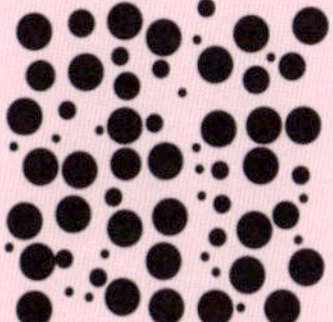

Second order stochastic printing
This features varied dot size and spacing to thoroughly mix things up and prevent the formation of moiré patterns.

FINISHING TERM

Paper used for printing. Different stocks have different properties that can affect the visual outcome of a printed piece, including varying lustre, absorbency and stiffness. Stock decisions increasingly take into account environmental issues such as the amount of recycled content; whether the paper was produced from sustainable forests and the practices adopted for the handling and disposal of the paper-making chemicals.

Acid-free
Paper that has a neutral pH of 7, or slightly higher, which is used for fine art and limited edition printing, for permanent records and in cases where contact with paper acidity could harm the documents.

Antique
A lightweight, sometimes bulky paper that is rough to the touch. Antique paper has a natural feel and random texture.

Chromo
A waterproof coated stock often used for covers and labels.

Newsprint
A cheap stock used for high-volume printing; its absorbency gives mediocre image reproduction.

Woodfree
Paper made without mechanical wood pulp.

Laid
Writing paper that has a watermark of fine lines running across the grain.

Uncoated

The most popular stock for commercial printing and office use.

Cast coated

Coated stock with a high-gloss finish for high-quality colour printing.

Art

High-brightness stock with a good printing surface used for colour printing and magazines.

Bible

Thin, white, opaque and absorbent. Used for printing bibles.

Bond

Paper with good strength, stiffness and aesthetic properties. These papers were originally used for printing bonds and share certificates.

Cotton

Paper made from cotton fibres. It has superior strength and durability compared to wood pulp paper; it absorbs ink well and produces a better printout than laser paper. Cotton paper is typically graded as 25%, 50% or 100% cotton.

Laid

Woodfree paper

Newsprint

PRINTING TERM | *Also called colour control bar*

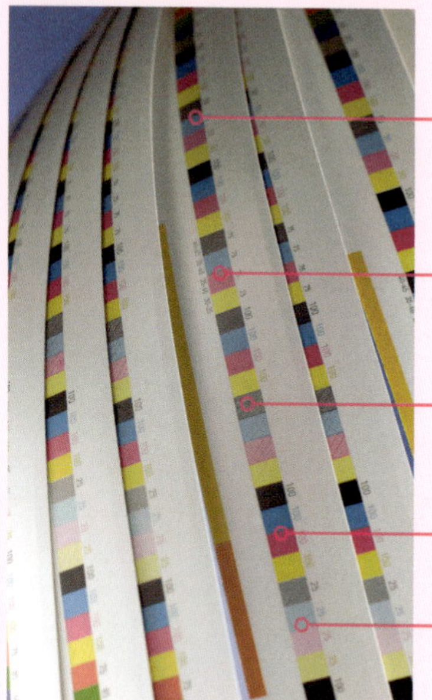

50% tints
50% tint patch tests whether tints are printing correctly.

75% tints
75% tint patch tests whether tints are printing correctly.

Dot gain test
Hatched squares or star targets test for dot gain.

Solid colours
Solid colours test for colour density.

25% tints
25% tint patch tests whether tints are printing correctly.

A bar of repeating predefined colours; it is printed along the full edge of a sheet for the press operator to check that the press is printing consistently. The striker bar (or colour control bar) includes additive primaries, subtractive primaries, tint patches, solid patches, three-colour neutral grey patches, star targets or hatched squares, RGB overprints and total area coverage (TAC) patches. A densitometer or loupe is used to check that colours are printing at the correct density.

☞ see Densitometer 70, Loupe 165, Printing 200, RGB 216

Stroke

Fill

Red stroke with gradient fill

The two distinct parts of a vector image. Stroke is the line or path used to draw the object; fill is the colour or pattern applied to an object. These can be treated separately for creative control, creating effects such as those shown above. A stroke can be set with different cap shapes, shown in blue below, and different joins, shown in magenta. These can be round, bevelled or square.

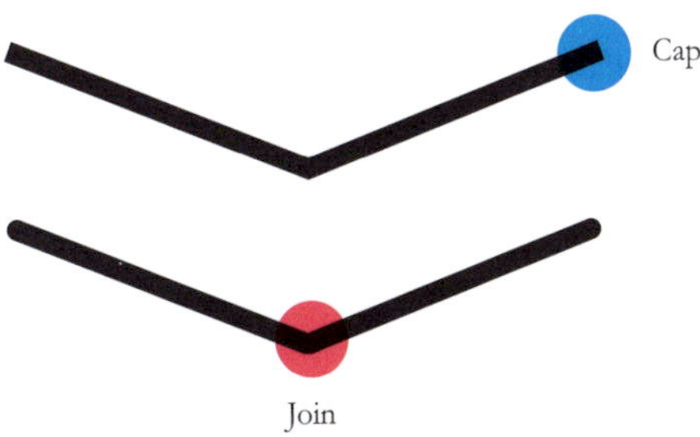

see Vector 275

DESIGN TERM

Pre-set text formatting styles. Many text-editing and layout programs include style sheets. Designers can create custom style sheets for a particular job or client or as part of a visual identity. Style sheets allow designers to quickly format text and apply the styles required for a job, either locally within an individual document or globally to a series of documents. A designer can also use style sheets to impart character and paragraph styles.

Character styles

Character style sheets control attributes that only relate to individual characters, such as size and colour.

Paragraph styles

These style sheets are used to alter attributes relating to paragraphs,such as leading and hyphenation, but they can also be used to control character attributes.

☛ see Hyphenation / Justification 136, Leading 156

Any material or surface that can hold an image. In printing, substrates are typically paper stocks but, thanks to the versatility of techniques such as screen printing, they can include plastic, fabric, metal and ceramics. The development of different substrates has seen an increase in the use of vinyl, for creating livery that is applied to vehicles.

Pictured are skateboards created by Unthink (who are keen skateboarders themselves): Emo badge collection; In and out of Rukos; and Scribble, which came with a marker pen.

see Paper 187, Screen Printing 223

PRINTING TERM

A TECHNIQUE OF PRINTING FROM A SINGLE COLOUR.

A SURPRINT USES THE TINT VALUES OF ONE COLOUR TO GIVE THE IMPRESSION OF TWO OR MORE COLOURS BEING USED.

SURPRINTS ARE OFTEN COMBINED WITH REVERSE OUTS, WHICH INTRODUCE THE STOCK COLOUR; AGAIN THIS CREATES THE ILLUSION THAT MORE COLOURS ARE BEING USED.

SURPRINTS ARE USEFUL WHEN YOU ARE RESTRICTED WITH COLOURS BUT WANT TO ADD A SENSE OF TEXTURE OR HIERACHY.

THIS PAGE, FOR INSTANCE, PRINTS IN ONE COLOUR, BUT THE ADDITION OF A SURPRINT AND REVERSE OUTS CREATES A MORE TEXTURED APPEARANCE.

☛ see Reverse Out 215

A projecting flap that extends beyond the dimension of the pages of a document. A tab can be part of a divider page or a sticky that is attached to the edge of a normal page. The two main types of tab are illustrated below:

Index cutting
Tabs cut or recessed into the page.

Tab cutting
Tabs cut into a divider that extends from the edge of the sheet.

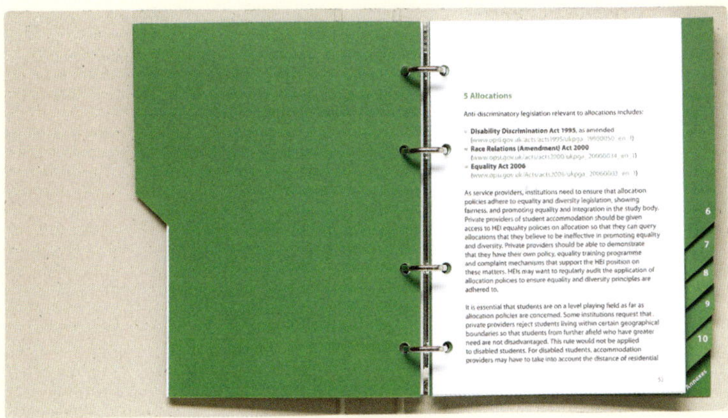

Pictured is a document created by Webb & Webb, which features green divider pages that have numbered tabs for easily identifying and accessing different parts of the document.

DESIGN TERM

A location set along the horizontal ruler to show where text should be aligned. A tab or tab stop provides a means for consistently aligning or indenting text as shown below.

This text is tabbed to the left so that each line
aligns a set distance from the left margin.

This text is set using a centre tab
whereby each line aligns to the
centre of the text block.

This text is set tabbed right
so that each line aligns
a set distance from the right margin.

A tab leader..can be used to fill the space between two columns that align on either side of a page, with periods or other characters, such as on the contents page of a book.

SCREEN TERM

A term or keyword attributed to a piece of information. Tagging helps aid retrieval and recognition. For example, image libraries give several tags to each image so that they can be found using different keywords. Webpages use meta tags in a similar way. A meta tag is an HTML code that describes webpage content. This information is used by search engines to index a page so that someone searching for specific content will be able to find it. The most important meta tag for search engine indexing is the description meta tag, which includes a brief description of the page.

see HTML 133

FINISHING TERM *Also called Smyth sewn binding*

A durable, high-quality binding method for both soft and hard cover books. Thread is sewn through the spine of individual folded signatures, passing through each page several times before it is tied off. The book block is further strengthened using flannel and adhesive on the spine. Thread sewing enhances the strength and quality of a book and enables it to lie open flat. The durable nature of this binding means it is used for books that will have heavy usage for an extended period of time, such as text books and coffee-table books.

see Binding 34, Signatures 234, Spine 240

FINISHING TERM

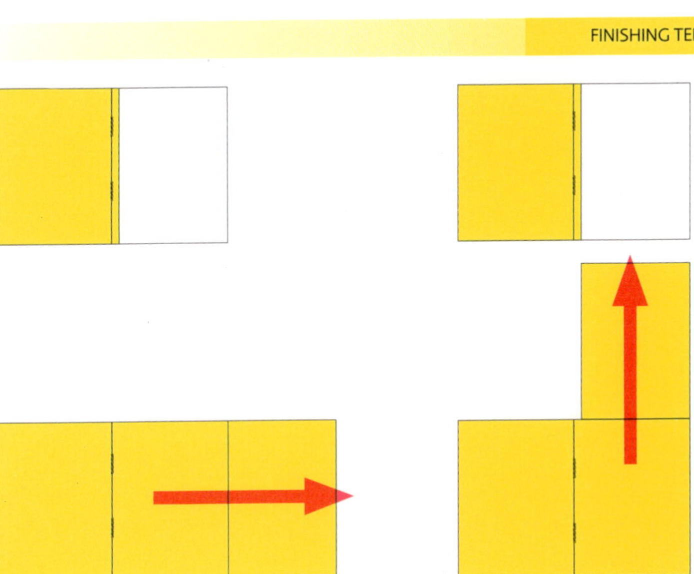

Throwout

Throw up

Sheets of folded paper bound into a publication to create an extra panel that folds out. A throw up typically folds out vertically above the page while a throwout folds out horizontally. A throwout is distinct from a gatefold, which is a four-panel folded sheet. Both methods provide extra space and are particularly useful for displaying outsize images or to enable an image to be printed to a larger scale. With either method, the panel bound into the publication has the same dimensions as its other pages, while the outer panel is slightly narrower to allow it to nest well when folded. These fold-outs are usually numbered with letters from the starting page, such as 32a and 32b for example, or they can be numbered sequentially with the pages.

see Folding 106, Gatefold 113

DESIGN TERM

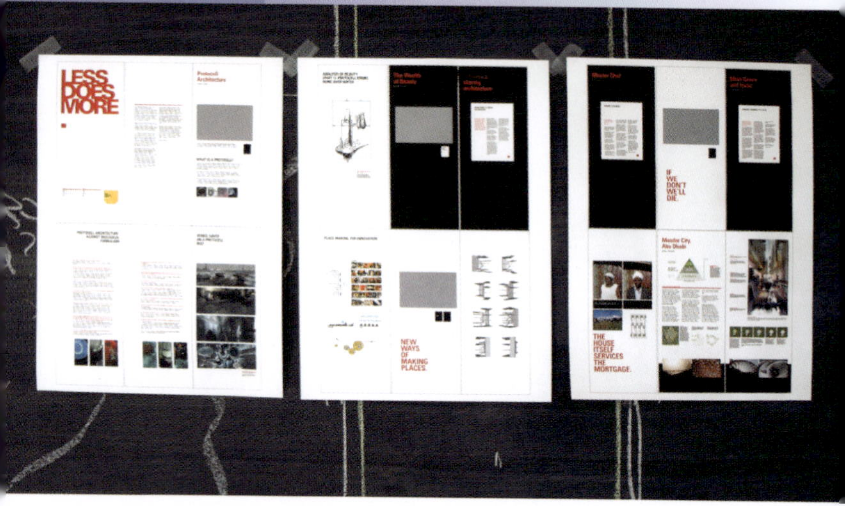

Small versions of a design, whether it be a book, exhibition or website. They are useful for enabling designers and clients to see the flow of a job, and also the overall impression of a design, but without the detail.

As an exercise, printing thumbnails enables you to ensure consistency of some items (certain sizes, hanging lines and so on), and variation of others (the pace of colour or the placement of images). This is helpful when it is difficult to appreciate how a run of pages will appear.

Thumbnails are also useful when checking the pagination or colour fall of a print job.

see Colour Fall 57, Pagination 185

DESIGN TERM

A continuous tone file format for lossless compression of images. TIFF (Tagged Image File Format) is a flexible method for storing halftones or colour bitmap images. It is cross-platform compatible, retains better image quality than a JPEG file and it is more suitable for printing. A TIFF file is also able to retain individual layers of the composite file.

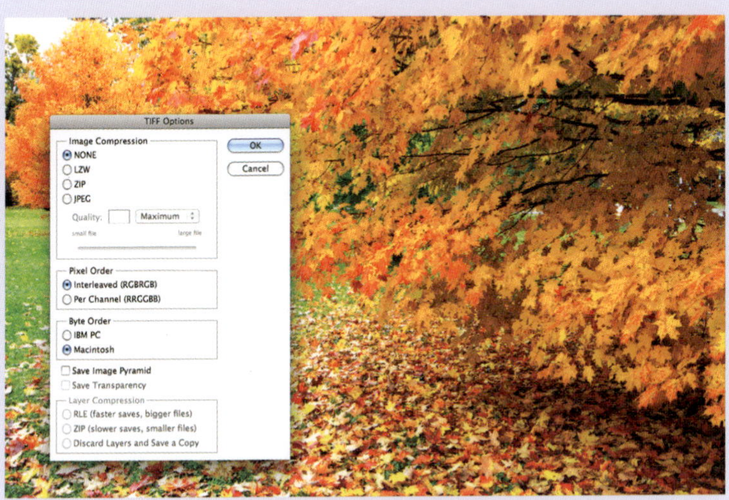

When saving TIFF files one has the option to compress the file size, for example using LSW or JPEG. One can also specify whether the TIFF is to be an IBM PC or Macintosh compatible file, although it is becoming more common for files to be cross-platform.

see Bitmap 36, Composite 59, Halftone 126, JPEG 148, Layers 155

DESIGN TERM

Tint refers to two distinct expressions. First, the white value of paper is expressed as a tint. The sheets of paper below are both white, but one has a yellow tint and the other is more blue. When choosing paper it is advisable to get samples for comparison, and also to consider how this will affect printing.

Secondly, tint refers to a specific value of a colour or pigment. When using tints in four-colour printing bear in mind that very high or very low values might not reproduce.

100%	90%	80%	70%	60%	50%	40%	30%	20%	10%	5%
100%	90%	80%	70%	60%	50%	40%	30%	20%	10%	5%

see Bitmap 36, Pigment 194, TIFF 259

T Tip-in and Tip-on

FINISHING TERM

Tip-in

A separate piece of stock bound into the pages of a publication. A tip-in is used to highlight, separate or organise different types of information. For example, colour plates on high-quality stock are commonly tipped into a publication printed on lower-quality stock. A tip-in is typically positioned between a publication's signatures, as this is an easy binding point. Pictured above is a tip-in created by February Design for *Next Level* magazine.

Tip-on

Not to be confused with a tip-in, a tip-on is a page or other element, such as a reply card, which is pasted on to the host page. Tip-ons can be of a temporary or a permanent nature.

DESIGN TERM

The halftone reproduction of an image using a black halftone and one or more colour halftones. In essence, a tonal image is akin to a black-and-white photograph in which the white tones have been replaced by one colour or a combination of colours. The use of two colours results in a duotone, three is a tritone and four a quadtone. Tonal images help create a level playing field between different images, particularly where they have different backgrounds, as colour detail is reduced. Image manipulation software includes filters that mimic the tonal effects achieved by photographic processes, such as warming and cooling, as shown here.

Warming filter 81

Warming filter 85

Cooling filter 80

Cooling filter 82

Various methods to adjust the spacing of text, words and letters to give a text block a more balanced feel.

Tracking adjusts the amount of space between characters.

Here, the tracking has been reduced, closing up the spaces between the letters.

In contrast, tracking can be opened up to introduce more space between letters.

As a general rule, the characters should be tracked so that they sit comfortably together, with enough space to be distinguishable but not so much that it is unclear which words they belong to.

Word spacing adjusts the amount of space between words. Different fonts have different word spacing values and some appear tighter than others.

Here, the word spacing has been closed up. This sets the separate words close together, which can make them more difficult to distinguish.

In contrast, word spacing can be opened up to clearly separate individual words.

DESIGN TERM *Also known as trannies*

A positive photographic image on a clear film base, which is viewed or projected by passing light through from behind. Photographs shot on reversal film are processed to produce transparencies or trannies. Reversal film is available in a wide range of sizes from 35mm to large formats such as 4 x 5 inches and 8 x 10 inches. Colour trannies are used for high-end print work; they give better colour reproduction compared to print film because slide film only has to go through development, and not printing. This means there is less opportunity for the developers to negatively affect the colour. Trannies may be supplied with notes to indicate which way round they are, as shown below right, to prevent them from being scanned back to front. Trannies can also be produced with a colour bar for reference when printing and scanning.

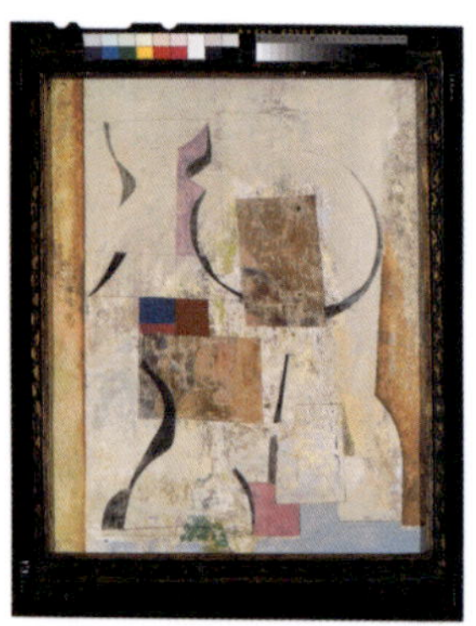

see Scanning 220

T Trapping

Also called spread and choke DESIGN TERM

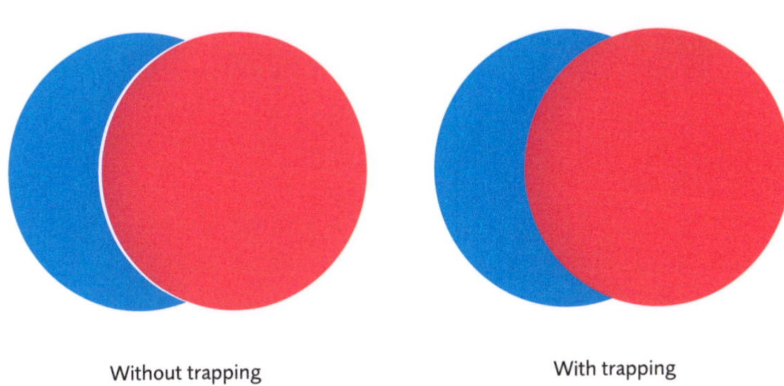

Without trapping With trapping

A technique that aids the registration of colour passes in a printing job by creating slight areas of overlap where two colours meet. Ink trapping helps avoid the presence of unsightly white spaces caused by misregistration, where inks that print as solid colours abut each other. There are two main ink trapping options: spread and choke. Most ink traps use spreading, whereby one object is made larger to spread into another. The magenta circle, top right, has been spread so that it overlaps with the cyan circle, making it slightly larger than the space it is to occupy. Standard practice is to spread a lighter object into a darker one. Choke reduces the size of the aperture in which an object will print, thereby 'choking' the space. Standard practice is to choke dark objects that sit inside a lighter one.

Trapping, which includes techniques like overprinting, is established at the design stage, so that the designer can control how different objects will print.

see Overprinting 182

PRINTING TERM

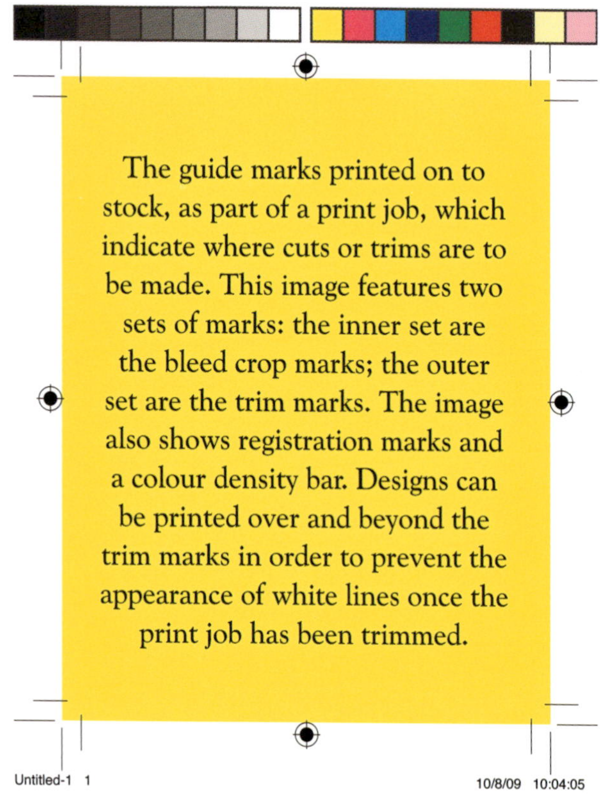
The guide marks printed on to stock, as part of a print job, which indicate where cuts or trims are to be made. This image features two sets of marks: the inner set are the bleed crop marks; the outer set are the trim marks. The image also shows registration marks and a colour density bar. Designs can be printed over and beyond the trim marks in order to prevent the appearance of white lines once the print job has been trimmed.
Untitled-1 1
10/8/09 10:04:05

see Bleed 38, Proofs 206

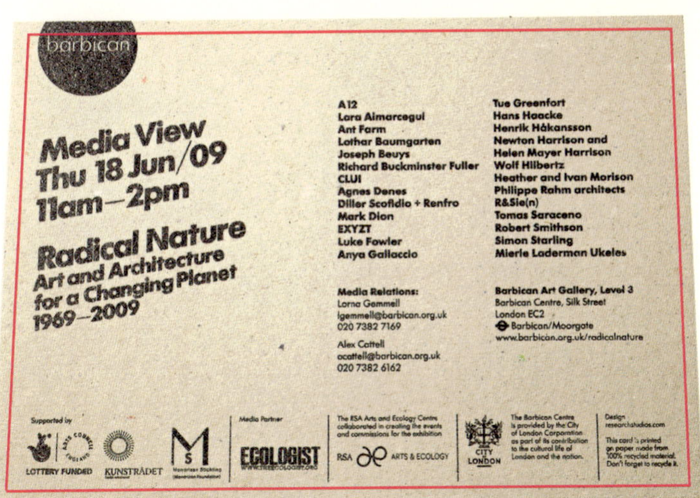

barbican
Media View
Thu 18 Jun/09
11am–2pm
Radical Nature
Art and Architecture
for a Changing Planet
1969–2009
A12
Lara Almarcegui
Ant Farm
Lothar Baumgarten
Joseph Beuys
Richard Buckminster Fuller
CLUI
Agnes Denes
Diller Scofidio + Renfro
Mark Dion
EXYZT
Luke Fowler
Anya Gallaccio
Tue Greenfort
Hans Haacke
Henrik Håkansson
Newton Harrison and
Helen Mayer Harrison
Wolf Hilbertz
Heather and Ivan Morison
Philippe Rahm architects
R&Sie(n)
Tomas Saraceno
Robert Smithson
Simon Starling
Mierle Laderman Ukeles
Media Relations:
Lorna Gemmell
lgemmell@barbican.org.uk
020 7382 7169
Alex Cattell
acattell@barbican.org.uk
020 7382 6162
Barbican Art Gallery, Level 3
Barbican Centre, Silk Street
London EC2
Barbican/Moorgate
www.barbican.org.uk/radicalnature
Supported by
LOTTERY FUNDED
KUNSTRÅDET
Media Partner
ECOLOGIST
The RSA Arts and Ecology Centre collaborated in creating the events and commissions for the exhibition
RSA
ARTS & ECOLOGY
CITY LONDON
The Barbican Centre is provided by the City of London Corporation as part of its contribution to the cultural life of London and the nation.
Design
researchstudios.com
This card is printed on paper made from 100% recycled material. Don't forget to recycle it.

The active space within a design that is surrounded by a safety margin for trimming. By leaving a safety margin around the type area, a designer can be sure that no part of the design will be lost when the job is trimmed, which is a possibility if text and graphic elements print to the edge of the stock. Designers typically leave 5–10mm as a safety margin. The example above, by Research Studios, has a border of space around the design, as indicated in magenta. Notice how the text within the black circle, which bleeds off the edge, is also positioned to the same safety margin.

see Bleed 38

DESIGN TERM

A typographical error or misspelling. Typos include, for example, transposed letters in a word, such as 'ua' in Pual instead of Paul, transposed words, missing words, repeatedrepeated words, upside-down characters and characters set in the wrong font, SIZE or colour.

see Orphans and Widows 180, Proof Correction Marks 204

DESIGN TERM

A print job that has no binding. Unbound print jobs include single flyers or pamphlets and more elaborate, folded pieces, such as the example shown here. Folding enables the printed sheet to be turned into a signature containing various pages or panels. Pictured is a brochure created by Mark Studio for the Environmental Business Pledge. The unbound nature of the document works well in this context; it conveys a sense of environmental care with the use of recycled paper and no binding materials.

see Folding 106, Signatures 234

PRINTING TERM

Also known as UCR

The replacement of cyan, magenta and yellow inks with black in the production of dark tones. UCR reduces the risk of offsetting and makes it easier for a printer to maintain colour balance. UCR uses less ink, which saves costs and enables quick drying time. However, as UCR can produce dull blacks, it may be necessary to add shiners to achieve rich black colours. When using UCR, the scanner is set to remove magenta and yellow from dark areas, to leave mostly black, with cyan added to compensate and bring out detail. The result is that a piece of dark coverage prints using two colours rather than four, as in the image above. A similar process is grey component replacement (GCR), which replaces some or all of the cyan, magenta and yellow inks with black, so that the colour is maintained.

see Shiners and Bouncers 232

PRINTING TERM

Printed items that do not form part of the print run. Unders are spoilage or defective copies; overs are good copies in excess of the required print run, which are kept as spares or file copies. Pictured are some overs of a brochure, created by February Design for London Wholesale Markets, which are used as file copies. Designers will usually request file copies as examples of jobs completed.

PRINTING TERM

A PRINTING PROCESS THAT INVOLVES PARTS OF THE DESIGN BEING ALTERED WITH EACH IMPRESSION. VARIABLE DATA PRINTING TYPICALLY INCLUDES PRINTING DIFFERENT NAMES, ADDRESSES OR SERIAL NUMBERS ON DOCUMENTS SUCH AS INVITES, RAFFLE TICKETS OR DIRECT MAIL.

see Impression 140, Printing 200

DESIGN TERM

Text set range right, range left
or centred has fixed spacing or widths
between words, which means that each
line of text spans a different amount of
space and has a ragged end.

Text set justified cannot have fixed spaces between words as the line endings would be ragged. This means that a designer has to decide on the maximum and minimum space allowed between words. If too little space is given, the words will seem to collide; too much and large spaces will open up in the text, increasing the likelihood of rivers. For this reason, when using justification, it is often necessary to allow words to break to make space setting easier to control.

see Hyphenation / Justification 136, Rivers 217

FINISHING TERM

A colourless coating that is applied to a printed piece to protect the substrate from wear or smudging. Applied as a spot varnish, it also acts to enhance the visual appearance of a design. Varnish may have gloss, satin or matte finishes.

Gloss A gloss varnish reflects light. It is frequently used to enhance the appearance of photographs or other graphic elements in brochures, as it adds to the sharpness and saturation of images.

Matte (or dull) Typically used with text-heavy pages to diffuse light, reduce glare and so increase readability. It creates a non-glossy, smooth finish to the printed page.

Satin (or silk) A middle option between the gloss and matte varnishes. It provides some highlight, but is not as flat as a matte finish.

Neutral The application of a basic, almost invisible coating that seals the printing ink without affecting the appearance of the job. It is often used to accelerate the drying of fast turnaround print jobs (such as leaflets) on matte and satin papers, upon which inks dry more slowly.

UV varnish A clear liquid that is applied like ink and cured instantly with ultraviolet light. It can provide either a gloss or a matte coating. UV varnish is increasingly used as a spot covering to highlight a particular image because it provides more shine than basic varnish.

Full-bleed UV The most common type of all-over UV coating, producing a high-gloss effect.

Spot UV The varnish is applied to highlight discrete areas of a printed design, both visually and by imparting a different texture. The effect of spot UV can be maximised when it is applied over matte-laminated printing.

Textured spot UV Textures can be created with spot UV varnish to provide an additional tactile quality to a printed piece.

Pearlescent A varnish that subtly reflects myriad colours to create a luxurious effect.

DESIGN TERM

An image that is defined by mathematical formulae rather than being built out of pixels. There are advantages and disadvantages to both formats.

Vector files are essentially 'drawn' files, which are mathematically rescaled to any size. This allows reproduction at any size without degradation in image quality. In essence, it is the information to reconstruct the drawing that is retained rather than the drawing itself. File sizes tend to be small, but this format isn't able to reproduce detailed photographic tone.

Raster images are built from pixels. This means they can reproduce photograhic tone. It also means they are of a fixed size and, if over-enlarged, they will appear pixelated, as shown below. Files sizes also tend to be high, as each pixel has to be individually 'remembered' or recorded.

Original image

A vector file can be enlarged to any size

A raster file, if over-enlarged, will look pixelated

see EPS 90, Raster 208

DESIGN TERM

Traditionally used to highlight or isolate the central portion of an image, with the image fading to the edges.

This has translated over to digital image manipulation in the form of a feather, which creates a soft edge to a path or selection. In the example above, the model has been isolated from the background using a rough feather effect. Portions within an image can be feathered or vignetted; in this case her face has been left full colour, while the remaining image has been duotoned.

☞ see Duotone 82, Image Manipulation 138

PRINTING TERM

A family of tough, flexible, shiny plastics that are often used for coverings and clothing. Vinyl can be applied to any surface and it is available in a wide range of finishes, such as metallic, shown here in an exhibition by Studio Myerscough; reflective, which appears to illuminate when lights fall upon it, for example from passing traffic; as well as anti-graffiti finishes. Vinyl is available with different levels of adhesivity, such as low tack for temporary applications and high tack, which is more permanent.

FINISHING TERM

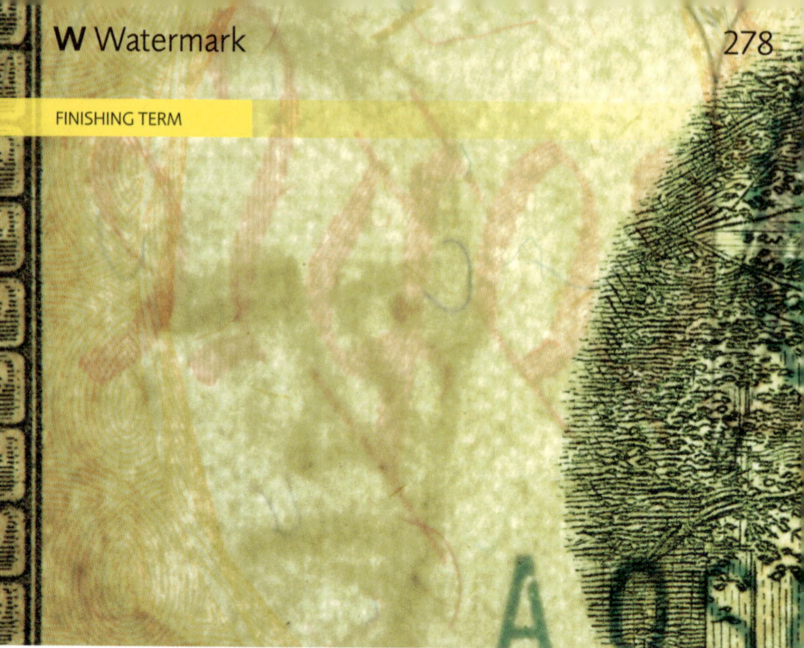

A translucent design impressed on paper stock, which is visible when the paper is held to the light. It is created during manufacture by a metal roller carrying the design. Watermarking was developed as a counterfeiting prevention measure, particularly on banknotes. It is also used to add a creative element or sign of quality to designs and products such as stationery.

Digital watermarks, often in the form of logo, are also added to photos, films and audio files to show the owner's copyright. Most photo-editing software includes a watermark function.

Pictured is a detail of a US 10 dollar bill featuring a watermark of US president Alexander Hamilton.

A high-volume, offset lithographic printing method that uses a continuous roll of paper. Once printed, the pages are separated and cut to size. Compared to sheet-fed printing, web offset printing provides greater economies of scale for large-volume print runs. Web offset printing may be heatset, meaning the ink is dried rapidly by forced-air heating; or coldset, which means that the ink dries by ordinary evaporation and absorption.

Economies of scale
A reduction in the cost per unit resulting from increased production. Economies of scale are realised where production increases and the cost of producing each additional unit falls.

W Web-safe Colours

SCREEN TERM

A group of 216 colours that can be reproduced by most computer displays. Web-safe colours have hexadecimal values, which represent the amount of red, green and blue (RGB) contained within each colour. Shown below are some of the most common web-safe colours and their hexadecimal codes.

Colour	Hexadecimal	Colour
aqua	#00FFFF	
gray (grey)	#808080	
navy	#000080	
silver	#C0C0C0	
black	#000000	
green	#008000	
olive	#808000	
teal	#008080	
blue	#0000FF	
lime	#00FF00	
purple	#800080	
white	#FFFFFF	
fuchsia	#FF00FF	
maroon	#800000	
red	#FF0000	
yellow	#FFFF00	

see RGB 216

SCREEN TERM

A limited selection of fonts that are likely to be available on most computers. If a computer does not have the exact font required, it substitutes one that may be quite different from that selected by the web author. However, using any of the fonts shown below virtually guarantees universal compatibility.

ANDALE MONO	ABCDEFGHIJKLMNOPQRSTUVWXYZ
ARIAL MT	ABCDEFGHIJKLMNOPQRSTUVWXYZ
ARIAL BLACK	**ABCDEFGHIJKLMNOPQRSTUVWXYZ**
COMIC SANS MS	ABCDEFGHIJKLMNOPQRSTUVWXYZ
COURIER NEW PS MT	ABCDEFGHIJKLMNOPQRSTUVWXYZ
GEORGIA	ABCDEFGHIJKLMNOPQRSTUVWXYZ
IMPACT	**ABCDEFGHIJKLMNOPQRSTUVWXYZ**
TIMES NEW ROMAN	ABCDEFGHIJKLMNOPQRSTUVWXYZ
TREBUCHET MS	ABCDEFGHIJKLMNOPQRSTUVWXYZ
VERDANA	ABCDEFGHIJKLMNOPQRSTUVWXYZ
WEBDINGS	

see Font / Typeface 108

SCREEN TERM

Terminology used to describe various facets of a website.

ActionScript
A scripting language used by the Adobe Flash Player platform to control its interactive events. ActionScript has similar syntax to JavaScript but functions only within Flash SWF files.

Netiquette
Generally accepted modes of good behaviour when communicating in the digital space, such as forums, email, blogs and chatrooms. Netiquette includes not abusing or flaming other users in an open forum; not sending or posting spam; and no writing in capitals.

Top Level Domain (TLD)
The highest hierarchical level of an internet site domain represented by what follows the dot in the address. Examples include .com, .co.uk, .net, .org and .biz.

Online
Being connected or logged in to the internet. Internet chat rooms and discussion forums usually show when a particular user is logged in and online. Online also describes any service accessible on the web.

Packet
A small piece of digital data. The internet uses TCP/IP technology to break down data into a number of packets to optimise data transmission. Data packets are reassembled at the destination.

Ping
A troubleshooting method used to check whether an internet connection exists.

Mirror site
A duplicate of a web or FTP site, which is used to balance the traffic load of a busy site.

Icon (shown above)
A graphic element with simple, easily recognisable characteristics, which represents an object, person or something else.

Back end
The software and/or database technology that sits on a server and drives the interactive activity, which is displayed on a web surfer using a web browser front end.

Front end
The visible part of a web browser that a user sees and interacts with; this is driven by the back-end software and database technology.

Home page
The root, top-most or first page that is generally viewable on a website. The home page is typically the one accessed by the site's web address.

Link
The area on a website that, when clicked, takes a user to another webpage, website or file download. A link is often a graphic or word.

see Back End / Front End 26, Hyperlink / Hypertext 135

DESIGN TERM

95 Black

95 Heavy

75 Bold

65 Medium

55 Roman

45 Light

35 Thin

25 Ultra Thin

The thickness of a typeface, ranging from very light to very heavy. The weight of a particular typeface will be identified in its name, which is expressed in different ways for different type families. The Univers type family uses numbers to identify its different weights while other families use descriptive names, such as heavy and thin, as shown.

see Font / Typeface 108

W Woodblock

Also called woodcut

PRINTING TERM

A relief printing method that involves pressing an inked block of wood, with an image carved into it, against a substrate. Woodblock or woodcut printing originated in China and is still used throughout Asia for printing textiles. Woodblock printing can result in some variation due to differences in ink coverage and pressure during the printing process. Other materials, such as lino, can be used as the block material.

Pictured is a printer's case containing different woodblock numerals.

☛ see Font / Typeface 108, Lino Cut Printing 163, Printing 200

PRINTING TERM

Two common printing impositions. Printing imposition is the arrangement of a print job, showing the sequence and position in which the pages will be printed before being cut, folded and trimmed. Work-and-turn and work-and-tumble both involve printing the pages of a section in two passes.

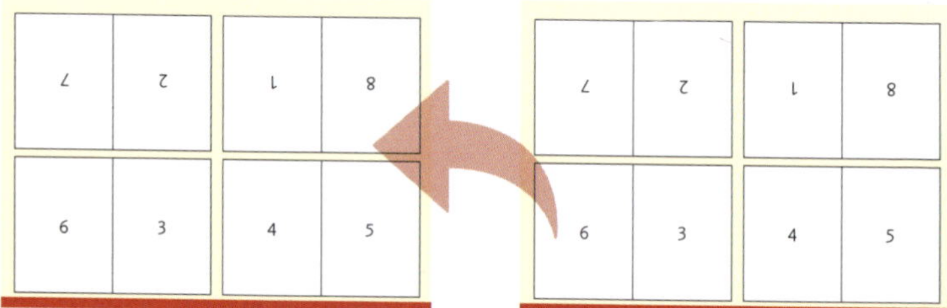

Work-and-turn

The coloured bar represents the gripper edge of the printing press, which holds the sheet to be printed. With work-and-turn, the sheet is turned 180 degrees to the side between passes. After both sides have been printed, the stock is cut and folded to make two identical eight-page sections.

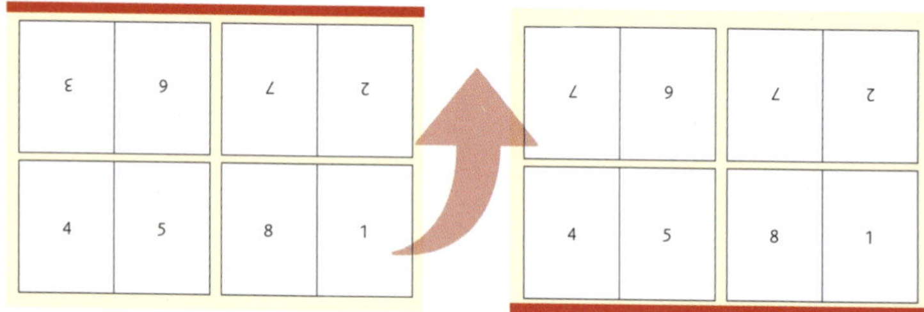

Work-and-tumble

Work-and-tumble sees the gripper edge change position from one side of the sheet to the other. The sheet is tumbled forward 180 degrees between passes. After both sides have been printed, the stock is cut and folded to make two identical eight-page sections.

FINISHING TERM

A z-shaped fold comprising two parallel folds. A z-bind can be used to bind two documents separately within the same publication or to provide a wraparound cover, as shown here, where the cover folds back upon itself.

Pictured is a design created by To The Point, which features a z-bind that holds the two discrete parts of the publication.

The Details

A range of standard complementary paper sizes specified by the ISO system, which cater for most common printing needs.

Size	Standard use
A0, A1	Posters and technical drawings, such as blueprints
A1, A2	Flip charts for meetings
A2, A3	Diagrams, drawings and large tables, spreadsheets, newspapers
A4	Magazines, letters, forms, leaflets, photocopiers, laser printers and general usage
A5	Notepads, diaries, books
A6	Postcards, books
A8	Playing cards

Size	mm
A0	841 x 1189
A1	594 x 841
A2	420 x 594
A3	297 x 420
A4	210 x 297
A5	148 x 210
A6	105 x 148
A7	74 x 105
A8	52 x 74
A9	37 x 52
A10	26 x 37

A range of standard complementary paper sizes specified by the ISO system, which cater for most common printing needs.

Size	Standard use
B4,	Newspapers
B5, B6	Books
B8	Playing cards

Size	mm
B0	1000 x 1414
B1	707 x 1000
B2	500 x 707
B3	353 x 500
B4	250 x 353
B5	176 x 250
B6	125 x 176
B7	88 x 125
B8	62 x 88
B9	44 x 62
B10	31 x 44

A variety of sizes that provide a range of different formats. Two factors affect the size of a book page: the size of the sheet of paper on which the book is printed and the number of times that sheet is folded before it is trimmed. Folio editions refer to books made of signatures that have been folded once; quarto editions are formed from signatures folded twice to make four leaves and eight pages; octavo editions are made from signatures folded three times to give eight leaves and 16 pages. Book sizes were originally based on standard paper sizes and so there exists a mathematical relationship between them: successive sizes are either twice or half the area and share one dimension. For example, a crown folio is 381 x 254mm. With another fold this becomes a crown quarto measuring 254 x 191mm, and a further fold creates a crown octavo measuring 191 x 127mm.

Bound book sizes	Abbreviation	H x W
1 Demy	16mo	143mm x 111mm
2 Demy	18mo	146mm x 95mm
3 Foolscap octavo	(8vo)	171mm x 108mm
4 Crown	(8vo)	191mm x 127mm
5 Large crown	8vo	203mm x 133mm
6 Demy	8vo	222mm x 143mm
7 Medium	8vo	241mm x 152mm
8 Royal	8vo	254mm x 159mm
9 Super royal	8vo	260mm x 175mm
10 Imperial	8vo	279mm x 191mm
11 Foolscap quarto	(4to)	216mm x 171mm
12 Crown	4to	254mm x 191mm
13 Demy	4to	260mm x 222mm
14 Royal	4to	318mm x 254mm
15 Imperial	4to	381mm x 279mm
16 Crown folio		381mm x 254mm
17 Demy folio		445mm x 286mm
18 Royal folio		508mm x 318mm
19 Music		356mm x 260mm

Standard paper sizes regulated by Canadian standard CAN 2-9.60M, which defines six P formats. These are rounded versions of the US sizes, based on two aspect ratios: 17/11=1.545 and 22/17=1.294. As per their US counterparts, the Canadian sizes lack a common height/width ratio enjoyed by the ISO standard paper sizes, and one cannot reduce or magnify from one format to the next without leaving a vacant margin.

Size	mm	ratio
PA1	560 x 840	2:3
PA2	420 x 560	3:4
PA3	280 x 420	2:3
PA4	210 x 280	3:4
PA5	140 x 210	2:3
PA6	105 x 140	3:4

A range of standard complementary paper sizes specified by the ISO system, which cater for most common printing needs. C series sizes have the addition of C10 and DL, which are standard envelope sizes.

Size	Standard use
C4, C5, C6	Envelopes to enclose A4 letters: unfolded (C4); folded once (C5); folded twice (C6)

Size	mm
C0	917 x 1297
C1	648 x 917
C2	458 x 648
C3	324 x 458
C4	229 x 324
C5	162 x 229
C6	114 x 162
C7/6	81 x 162
C7	81 x 114
C8	57 x 81
C9	40 x 57
C10	28 x 40
DL	110 x 220

Deutsches Institut für Normung (DIN) is the German Institute for Standardisation; a member body of the ISO. DIN has been influential in the establishment of many standards used around the world, including paper standards. Perhaps the most well-known is DIN 476, the standard that became the ISO A and B paper sizes in 1922, and subsequently adopted as ISO 216 in 1975. DIN 476 has two main differences from its international successor. DIN 476 provides an extension to formats larger than A0, which is indicated by a prefix. These are 2A0, which is twice the area of A0; and 4A0, which is four times the size of A0. DIN standard DIN 824 outlines a method for folding standard AO paper size down to the A4 size. This folding method produces a 20mm margin on one layer that can be hole-punched for filing so that a document can be unfolded and folded again without being removed. This method also means that the label field located in the bottom left-hand corner of technical drawings ends up on top of the folded page in the file.

A standard system for envelope sizes provided by the ISO standards system. The DL format (dimension lengthwise according to ISO 269) is the most widely used business letter format, but its dimensions are somewhat outside the ISO system, with equipment manufacturers complaining that it is a little too small for reliable automatic envelope fulfilment. As such, the C6/C5 format was developed as an alternative. The ISO C series provides standard envelope sizes but there is no international standard for window envelopes and matching letterhead layouts.

Format Size [mm]	Content	Format
C6 114 x 162	A4 folded twice =	A6
DL 110 x 220	A4 folded twice =	1/3 A4
C6/C5 114 x 229	A4 folded twice =	1/3 A4
C5 162 x 229	A4 folded once =	A5
C4 229 x 324	A4	
C3 324 x 458	A3	
B6 125 x 176	C6 envelope	
B5 176 x 250	C5 envelope	
B4 250 x 353	C4 envelope	
E4 280 x 400	B4	

Outdoor media comes in a vast range of sizes from A4 posters to giant billboards. Scale is obviously the defining factor in outdoor media as designs have to catch attention from a distance. Although outdoor media can be produced at any size there are several standard sizes. The first is a single sheet called D-size, which is used by architects for oversize drawings. This is a standard print size for reproduction, which corresponds to the double crown sheet size. The common poster sizes are given here in millimetres (mm), with height followed by width.

Single sheet Size: 762 x 508mm
The basic large format unit in portrait orientation.

6 sheet Size: 1524 x 1016mm
This is the most widespread outdoor format, in portrait orientation. Its compact size means it can be used where space is at a premium, such as bus-stops.

12 sheet Size: 1524 x 3048mm
The 12-sheet poster is a landscape format.

48 sheet Size: 3048 x 6096mm
The standard billboard size gives 200ft² of presentation space in landscape orientation and gives a high level of message frequency.

96 sheet Size: 3048 x 12192mm
Following 48 sheet, this is the second most common billboard format, also in landscape orientation, giving 400ft² of presentation space. It has the same vertical dimension as the 48-panel billboard.

European Size: 3048 x 3962mm
A square format popular in Europe but with the same vertical dimension as the 48-sheet and 96-sheet billboards.

Golden Square Size: 6096 x 6096mm
A square format, typically illuminated at night, which helps improve viewer attention by breaking the boundary of standard rectangular dimensions and through its sheer scale.

Typographical characters have an array of attributes and forms that are described through a variety of different terms, in much the same way as the different names for every part of the human body.

Apex
The point formed at the top of a character such as 'A', where the left and right strokes meet.
Arm
A horizontal stroke that is open at one or both ends, as seen on the 'T', 'F' and 'K' as well as the upstroke on the 'K' and 'Y'. Also called *bar*.
Ascenders and descenders
An ascender is the part of a letter that extends above the x-height; the descender falls below the baseline.
Barb
A sharp-pointed serif.
Beak
The serif form at the end of an arm.
Bowl
The part of a character that encloses a space in circular letterforms such as 'O' and 'e'. The bowl may be closed or open.
Bracket The transitional shape, connecting the stem and the serif.
Chin The angled terminal of a 'G'.
Counter The space inside a bowl as found on 'e', 'a' and other letters.
Cross stroke / crossbar The horizontal stroke on the characters 'A', 'H', 'T', 'e', 'f', and 't' that intersects the central stem.
Crotch
The inner point at which two angled strokes meet.
Ear
A small stroke extending from the right side of the bowl of a 'g' or protruding from the stem of letters such as 'r' and 'f'.
Finial
An ornamental terminal stroke at the top of characters such as 'a' and 'f'.

Leg
The lower, possibly downward-sloping stroke of a letter. Sometimes also used for the tail of the 'Q'.
Ligature
Typically a crossbar or arm that extends across a pair of letters to join them.
Link
A stroke that joins two other letter parts such as the bowls of a double-storey 'g'.
Loop
The bowl formed by the tail of a double-storey 'g'.
Serif
A small stroke at the end of a main vertical or horizontal stroke.
Shoulder
The curved stroke leading into the leg of an 'h' or 'n'.
Spine
A left-to-right curving stroke in 'S' and 's'.
Spur
The terminal to a stem of a rounded letter.
Stem
The main vertical or diagonal stroke of a letter.
Stress
The orientation, or slant, of a curved character.
Swash
An elongated curved entry or exit stroke.
Tail
The descending stroke on a 'Q', 'K' and 'R'. The descenders on 'g', 'j', 'p', 'q' and 'y' may also be called tails, as can the loop of the 'g'.
Terminal
The end of a stroke, which may take several forms such as acute, flared, convex, concave and rounded.
Vertex
The angle formed at the bottom of a letter where the left and right strokes meet, such as in 'M'.

The range of book sizes for publishing in the USA, as used by the American Library Association.

Book formats and corresponding sizes

Name	Abbreviations	Book size in inches	Size in cm
Folio	2 or Fo	19 x 12	48.2 x 30.5
Quarto	4 or 4to	12 x 9.5	30.5 x 24.1
Octavo	8 or 8vo	9 x 6	22.8 x 15.2
Duodecimo or Twelvemo	12 or 12mo	7.4 x 5	18.7 x 12.7
Sextodecimo or Sixteenmo	16 or 16mo	6.75 x 4	17.1 x 10.1
Octodecimo or Eighteenmo	18 or 18mo	6.5 x 4	16.5 x 10.1
Trigesimo-secundo or Thirty-twomo	32 or 32mo	5.5 x 3.5	14 x 9
Sexagesimo-quarto or Sixty-fourmo	64 or 64mo	3 x 2	7.6 x 5

Standard paper sizes regulated by American National Standards. As with the ISO paper standard system, the US standard maintains a relationship in the size ratios. However, while the ISO system enjoys a uniform aspect ratio the US system alternates between two: 17/11=1.545 and 22/17=1.294, which means one cannot reduce or magnify from one format to the next without leaving a vacant margin. The most commonly used sizes are letter, legal, executive and ledger/tabloid.

Size	mm	in	ratio
ANSI A	279 x 176	11 x 8½	1.2941
ANSI B	432 x 279	17 x 11	1.5455
ANSI C	559 x 432	22 x 17	1.2941
ANSI D	864 x 559	33 x 22	1.5455
ANSI E	1118 x 864	44 x 34	1.2941

The various pre-press processes detailed in this book are the means through which a design idea is turned into a physical printed product. This volume has attempted to explain the key elements of those pre-press production processes to provide a better understanding of the vocabulary; this will improve communication between design, print and finishing professionals, which contributes to the final result appearing as it was conceived by the design team.